Andrew Jackson

Andrew Jackson was the seventh president of the United States. Known as "Old Hickory," he was the first president who championed the rights of the 'common man'. Originally from the frontier, he was known for being rough in speech and mannerisms and his fierce temper. After making his name as a general fighting the Creek Indians in the Battle of Horseshoe Bend and the British in the Battle of New Orleans, he entered politics, resulting in the creation of the modern Democratic Party. However, Jackson is best known today for the harsh stand he took on Indian Removal.

In this concise account, John Belohlavek recounts what made Jackson such a magnetic and controversial figure in his own time. Separating truth from legend, *Andrew Jackson: Principle and Prejudice* shows how deeply Andrew Jackson's actions and policies as president have affected the modern United States.

John M. Belohlavek is Professor of History at the University of South Florida.

ROUTLEDGE HISTORICAL AMERICANS

SERIES EDITOR: PAUL FINKELMAN

Routledge Historical Americans is a series of short, vibrant biographies that illuminate the lives of Americans who have had an impact upon the world. Each book includes a short overview of the person's life and puts that person into historical context through essential primary documents, written both by the subjects and about them. A series website supports the books, containing extra images and documents, links to further research, and, where possible, multi-media sources on the subjects. Perfect for including in any course on American history, the books in the Routledge Historical Americans series show the impact everyday people can have upon the course of history.

Woody Guthrie: Writing America's Songs
Ronald D. Cohen

Frederick Douglass: Reformer and Statesman
L. Diane Barnes

Thurgood Marshall: Race, Rights, and the Struggle for a More Perfect Union
Charles L. Zelden

Harry S. Truman: The Coming of the Cold War
Nicole L. Anslover

John Winthrop: Founding the City upon a Hill
Michael Parker

John F. Kennedy: The Spirit of Cold War Liberalism
Jason K. Duncan

Bill Clinton: Building a Bridge to the New Millennium
David H. Bennett

Ronald Reagan: Champion of Conservative America
James H. Broussard

Laura Ingalls Wilder: American Writer on the Prairie
Sallie Ketcham

Benjamin Franklin: American Founder, Atlantic Citizen
Nathan R. Kozuskanich

Brigham Young: Sovereign in America
David Vaughn Mason

Mary Lincoln: Southern Girl, Northern Woman
Stacy Pratt McDermott

Oliver Wendell Holmes, Jr.: Civil War Soldier, Supreme Court Justice
Susan-Mary Grant

Belle La Follette: Progressive Era Reformer
Nancy C. Unger

Harriet Tubman: Slavery, the Civil War, and Civil Rights in the Nineteenth Century
Kristen T. Oertel

Muhammad Ali: A Man of Many Voices
Barbara L. Tischler

Andrew Jackson: Principle and Prejudice
John M. Belohlavek

Sojourner Truth: Prophet of Social Justice
Isabelle Kinnard Richman

ANDREW JACKSON
PRINCIPLE AND PREJUDICE

JOHN M. BELOHLAVEK

NEW YORK AND LONDON

http://www.routledge.com/cw/historicalamericans

First published 2016
by Routledge
711 Third Avenue, New York, NY 10017

and by Routledge
2 Park Square, Milton Park, Abingdon, Oxon, OX14 4RN

Routledge is an imprint of the Taylor & Francis Group, an informa business

© 2016 Taylor & Francis

The right of John Belohlavek to be identified as author of this work has been asserted by him in accordance with sections 77 and 78 of the Copyright, Designs and Patents Act 1988.

All rights reserved. No part of this book may be reprinted or reproduced or utilised in any form or by any electronic, mechanical, or other means, now known or hereafter invented, including photocopying and recording, or in any information storage or retrieval system, without permission in writing from the publishers.

Trademark notice: Product or corporate names may be trademarks or registered trademarks, and are used only for identification and explanation without intent to infringe.

Library of Congress Cataloging-in-Publication Data
Names: Belohlavek, John M., author.
Title: Andrew Jackson : principle and prejudice / John M. Belohlavek.
Description: New York, NY : Routledge, 2016. | Series: Routledge historical Americans | Includes bibliographical references.
Identifiers: LCCN 2015041830 | ISBN 9780415844857 (hardback) | ISBN 9780415844864 (pbk.) | ISBN 9780203749517 (ebk)
Subjects: LCSH: Jackson, Andrew, 1767–1845. | Presidents—United States—Biography. | United States—Politics and government—1829–1837.
Classification: LCC E382.B45 2016 | DDC 973.5/6092—dc23
LC record available at http://lccn.loc.gov/2015041830

ISBN: 978-0-415-84485-7 (hbk)
ISBN: 978-0-415-84486-4 (pbk)
ISBN: 978-0-203-74951-7 (ebk)

Typeset in Minion and Scala Sans
by Apex CoVantage, LLC

To the students over the decades in the Age of Jackson.

Contents

Acknowledgments — xi

Introduction — 1

PART I
Andrew Jackson — 5

Chapter 1	Youth on the Frontier (1767–1811)	7
Chapter 2	The Border Captain: British and Indian Threats (1812–1818)	23
Chapter 3	The Road to the Presidency (1819–1828)	39
Chapter 4	The White House Years: First Term (1829–1833)	61
Chapter 5	The White House Years: Second Term (1833–1837)	81
Chapter 6	Retirement at the Hermitage (1837–1845)	105
Chapter 7	The Jackson Legacy	116

PART II
Documents **121**

Documents 123

Bibliography 145

Index 147

ACKNOWLEDGMENTS

Historians who study antebellum America develop their own views of Andrew Jackson. As a central figure in the unfolding of nationhood, he is that immovable object that must be considered. I want to thank the staff of Routledge Press, from Kim Guinta to Dan Finaldi, and editor Paul Finkelman for giving me the opportunity to develop my own particular Jackson. There are widely varying ways to present the controversial "Old Hickory" and I have attempted to achieve a balance in this brief volume. My task has been aided immeasurably by the thoughtful comments and well-considered criticisms of editor Finkelman, Paul Bergeron, Justus Doenecke, Nat Jobe, and Gary Mormino. Susan Turner and her assistant, Jake, added their own keen eyes to each chapter. The careful reading of friends and colleagues improved this work, but, of course, they bear none of the responsibility for any errors in content or interpretation.

Introduction

Presidents who are highly regarded for their performance in office remain popular with the American people. George Washington, Thomas Jefferson, Abraham Lincoln, and Franklin D. Roosevelt highlight such a list. Within the past generation, each has been soundly criticized by scholars for their political or personal failings, but have retained their popularity. We witness, for example, the hundreds of thousands of visitors each year who view the monuments in their honor in Washington, DC, or crowd their homes in the summer heat. We take for granted their images on coinage and currency, their names on towns and schools.

Andrew Jackson shares in this celebrity status. The Hermitage, his plantation house outside Nashville, Tennessee, entertains almost 200,000 visitors annually. The capital of Mississippi bears his name, and the city of New Orleans's most prominent square features a dramatic statue of the victorious general astride his horse. His picture stares out from the $20 note. Yet Jackson is clearly controversial. Discussions were held in 2015 about removing "Old Hickory's" face from the currency and replacing him with a woman or ethnic/racial minority. Many local chapters of the Democrat party have changed the name of their annual celebratory dinner from "Jefferson-Jackson" to "Kennedy-King."

Recent presidents, such as Ronald Reagan and Bill Clinton, generate predictably strong feelings among their partisans. The emotive response generated by Jackson, who has been dead for over 150 years, however, is unusual. His reputation with the American public and within the academic community provides a fascinating case study in how society applies its evolving value constructs to historical figures and events. Popular culture has not ignored Andrew Jackson. During the 1950s, rising star Charlton Heston assumed the hero's role in two films that celebrated the virtues of

"Old Hickory." *The President's Lady* (1953), a romantic tale of love and scandal, traced the courtship and marriage of Jackson and Rachel Donelson Robards through his White House victory in 1828 and her ensuing untimely death. *The Buccaneer* (1958) was the saga of the life and loves of Caribbean pirate Jean Lafitte. The movie focuses, however, upon the Battle of New Orleans in January 1815 and Lafitte's sometimes contentious relationship with Jackson (played once again by Heston) as they prepared to face a powerful British army in the most memorable encounter of the War of 1812. The film's popularity was boosted by a song entitled "The Battle of New Orleans" by country and western artist Johnny Horton. Although the melody had been written two decades earlier, the 1959 version amazingly became the number one song in the nation that year. Anyone over the age of sixty-five knows the words and will eagerly sing it. The patriotic, honorable, and unflappable Jackson fitted in perfectly with the politics and morality of the Cold War decade.

More recently, Jackson has undergone greater scrutiny in an age of differing priorities and greater social concern. Jackson's ownership of slaves and generally hostile relationship with Native Americans—from wars against them to their removal to the West—has prompted a harsher examination of him before and during his presidency. The History Channel produced a critical biography (2007) and PBS followed up in 2008 with a study narrated by famed actor Martin Sheen entitled *Andrew Jackson: Good, Evil, and the Presidency*. On stage, Michael Friedman and Alex Timbers transformed him into an indie-rock star in *Bloody, Bloody Andrew Jackson*. The rather profane, irreverent musical debuted in 2006, was performed for several years, and was generally lauded by critics and receptive audiences. Its controversial approach to Jackson, Indians, and politics prompted extensive controversy. As productions emerged at universities and in local theaters protests followed. At Stanford, the complaints resulted in the cancellation of an on-campus performance.

Over several centuries, biographers have similarly transformed Jackson. Commencing with a defense of the general's actions in the Creek War and War of 1812, John Reid and John Henry Eaton marshaled a strong case for their hero in the 1817 study, *The Life of Andrew Jackson*. His reputation rose and fell into the twentieth century, although the criticism had little to do with slavery or Indian removal. Jackson was generally credited with encouraging the participation of the masses in American democracy. During the late nineteenth-century, immigration, corruption, and political radicalism clouded the landscape, and scholars debated whether the involvement of "the people" really was a good idea. The struggle over Jackson remained unrelenting. As late as the 1970s, consummate Jackson scholar Robert

V. Remini penned a three-volume study (1977–1984) largely defending his subject. Concurrently, Michael Paul Rogin's *Fathers and Children: Andrew Jackson and the Subjugation of the American Indian* (1975) and James C. Curtis's *Andrew Jackson and the Search for Vindication* (1976) revealed a psychologically troubled individual whose driving forces were far more personal than patriotic. More recently, accomplished scholars have given us Jackson studies large and small, from Andrew Burstein (2003), H.W. Brands (2005), Sean Wilentz (2005), Mark Cheathem (2013), and Jon Meacham's (2008) Pulitzer Prize-winning account of Jackson's presidency.

Each of these historians offers a particular version of Andrew Jackson. This study is neither as comprehensive as Remini's study, nor as thematically-focused as Rogin's. The goal is, in part, to dispel clichéd references that seem to invariably come up in classes on the Age of Jackson. For example, while Jackson was clearly instrumental in the removal of the southeastern tribes, he did not initiate or oversee the removal of the Cherokee in 1838 on the "Trail of Tears." He departed the White House in the winter of 1837. Nor did Jackson defy the Supreme Court ruling which offered hope to the Indians by remarking, "John Marshall made his decision, now let him enforce it." This legendary comment was crafted almost thirty years later by New York *Tribune* editor Horace Greeley. Jackson also did not give the vote to the "common man." While he marshaled the suffrage of white males into his new political party in the 1820s, the ballot was extended by the states in their revised constitutions, not by the federal government.

Beyond dispelling clichés, this volume presents a complex individual. A man of common background, rough edges, and little education, violent, proud and unyielding, he defies easy categorization. A western man and a southern gentleman, he was a product of humble origins on the Carolina frontier and a member of the Tennessee plantation aristocracy. He claimed the mantle of states' rights and a belief in the freedom and power of the individual from Jefferson, but also passionately defended the Union and threatened civil war during the nullification crisis with South Carolina.

As a man of principle, he embraced the notion of a country with an unlimited destiny. His dedication to an agrarian society and trust in the virtue of the people resonated powerfully in his generation. That faith transferred to a confidence in the creation of a mass majoritarian democracy engaging the average citizen as a substitute for a more elitist representative government. Jackson could then build a political party, expand the power of the presidency, and vociferously argue for the permanence of the Union with the assurance that he had the devotion and support of the people. As a man of prejudice, he was no social liberal or believer in an egalitarian society that offered rights or privileges for women, African Americans, or Indians. His prejudices reached beyond the nation's borders to Europe and Latin America. The parochial and culturally limited Jackson had little regard for anyone who was not white or American.

Today, as two centuries ago, Andrew Jackson angers and infuriates, arouses and inspires. This volume invites the reader to explore the varied aspects of the career and persona of a multi-faceted and complicated figure who rightfully belongs in this series on "Historical Americans."

PART I

ANDREW JACKSON

CHAPTER 1

YOUTH ON THE FRONTIER (1767–1811)

Laughter drowned out the shouts of encouragement as a tall, lean bolt of lightning exploded across the flat open grass, focused on the finish line a quarter mile ahead. At the start, his rival, heavier and more slow-footed, was given a lead of half the course's distance. This advantage was compromised, however, by the weight of the man he carried on his back! Amidst cheering and merriment, this friendly rivalry played out in 1787 on the North Carolina frontier, and offers significant insight into the subject of this biography. Young Andrew Jackson challenged his friend and fellow law student Hugh Montgomery to race. This common amusement in rural America was frequently enhanced by wagering on the contest. Amazingly, and to the surprise and delight of a number of the bettors, Jackson won by two yards.

   This duel was not only a microcosm of the personality and character of the youthful Jackson, but also informs us about the man he would become. By the age of 20, Jackson had grown into the 6 foot 1 inch, 140-pound frame that he maintained throughout his life. Sinewy and strong, his physical energy and courage melded with will power and determination that his rivals underestimated at their peril. Jackson balanced the resilient aspects of his character with a reckless streak that often unnecessarily placed him on life's edge. Gambling, including cards, horses, and cockfighting, was risky, but he won more often than not. His teenage lust for life included a seemingly insatiable appetite for women and alcohol. He took dancing very seriously, and rarely turned down an invitation to a soirée. The girls were charmed by his elegant manner as well as his sharp features, reddish hair, freckles, and penetrating blue eyes. Historian Robert V. Remini sums up the teenage Jackson by noting that the locals already considered him a "rake." In two decades, Andrew Jackson had travelled less than one hundred miles from the back country of South Carolina to Salisbury, North Carolina, yet the journey was life-changing. He would never return.[1]

The chosen path of Andrew Jackson, based upon his family history, would perhaps appear predictable to a contemporary psychologist or social worker. Jackson never knew his father, and his mother and siblings died when he had barely entered his teens. His Scotch-Irish parents, Andrew and Elizabeth, along with brothers Hugh and Robert, had departed Northern Ireland in 1765, seeking opportunity along the American frontier. They settled into the "Waxhaws," a western area disputed between North and South Carolina, chosen largely because Elizabeth's four sisters had already established themselves with their families nearby. The Jacksons worked hard to make their two hundred acres productive, until Andrew died suddenly of unknown causes in March 1767. Painfully, Elizabeth gave birth on March 15 to her third son, named for her husband, just days later.

With no adult male to manage the farm, Elizabeth and her sons were obliged to move in with her sister, Jane Crawford, who lived on a plantation about ten miles distant. The more prosperous Crawfords owned slaves, and their large house easily accommodated the four new additions. Elizabeth paid fourteen pounds in 1770 for the title to their own farm to be placed in her sons' names, though the boys grew up with Uncle James, Aunt Jane, and their eight children. Jane had become an invalid, so Elizabeth's presence as active overseer of the upbringing of eleven offspring met the needs of everyone involved.[2]

Elizabeth determined that Andrew was the brightest of her boys, the chosen one who would receive the best education and become a Presbyterian minister. Accordingly, he benefited from the tutelage of William Humphries at the Waxhaw Church, reading and writing by the age of eight. In a region where literacy was at a premium, young Andrew gained standing for his intelligence. Indeed, he was called upon in the summer of 1776 to read the difficult phrasing of the Declaration of Independence to his eager neighbors. The South managed to avoid the ravages of the American Revolution for the next several years and a persistent Elizabeth kept up the educational pressure on her son, sending him to a classical boarding school where he could learn Latin. A rather apathetic Andrew preferred to spend his time mastering more fascinating and practical pursuits, specifically muskets, horses, and cockfighting. Exhibiting a wiry build and fearless demeanor, he rapidly garnered a reputation among his peers for a hair-trigger temper, shameless cursing, and a willingness to relentlessly fight much larger comrades. In his early teens, Jackson already held an exaggerated sense of honor which he maintained throughout his lifetime. His "shrill" voice and tendency to slobber when he spoke prompted barbs and cruel jests from his peers. Jackson's response was certain and violent.

By 1779, the British had taken Savannah, Georgia, and the war moved swiftly into South Carolina, where Royal forces threatened Charleston. Captain Robert Crawford officered a Waxhaw militia company, including 16-year-old Hugh Jackson, which rushed into action in defense of the capital. While the battle of Stono Ferry in June was a nominal Redcoat victory, Charleston survived and the casualties were few. Sadly, Hugh was among them, dying soon thereafter of heat and exhaustion.

The British launched a new offensive in the spring of 1780, and on May 12, Charleston fell. Tories loyal to King George III joined with the British forces of Sir Henry Clinton, Lord Cornwallis, and cavalry commander, Colonel Banastre Tarleton, to battle Patriots committed to the rebellion in a civil war that pitted family against family. As Tarleton understated in his memoir of the campaign, "The sentiments of the inhabitants did not correspond with his lordship's expectations." The conflict quickly moved to the Waxhaws, where the Redcoats successfully drove the Americans out of South Carolina. Andrew, now 13, and 16-year-old brother Robert, joined the fray, signing up with Major William Davie's dragoons. This was guerrilla warfare, and Andrew knew the backcountry, rode well, and could shoot. Davie gave him a pistol and made him a messenger. Jackson watched the ebb and flow of combat in the chaotic region, and witnessed his first action on August 6, 1780, as the Americans won a minor victory at Hanging Rock.

Unfortunately for the rebels, a week later Cornwallis crushed General Horatio Gates at Camden. Elizabeth wisely fled with her sons to North Carolina and safety. The British showed little clemency to those civilians sympathetic to the Revolution and little mercy to soldiers who surrendered. The heavy-handed Redcoat treatment of colonials and mangled bodies of wounded Patriots made an enduring impression on the young Jackson.

Throughout the fall and winter of 1780–1781, warfare, erratic and brutal, consumed the countryside. The revolutionaries rallied, successfully challenging the British at King's Mountain and Cowpens, inflicting heavy casualties at Guilford Courthouse. When Cornwallis pressed on into the interior of North Carolina in February 1781, Elizabeth Jackson determined that she and her boys could return home. Her decision was fraught with danger. The Waxhaws remained a no man's land lacking courts, laws, or protection. Andrew and Robert rejoined the militia, sniping at the British and their Tory allies in ugly small group contests that continued well into the spring.

Following Jackson's only skirmish in April, a Tory revealed the whereabouts of the brothers, who sought food and shelter at the home of a local Patriot. Trapped inside with the family, the boys had no choice but surrender. The British trashed the house, destroying furniture and tearing bed linens and clothing to shreds. Seeking total humiliation, the commanding officer ordered Andrew to clean his muddy boots. Jackson defiantly refused, prompting a curse and a blow to the head from the Redcoat's sword. Fortunately, the boy raised his left arm to defend himself and the sabre glanced off his forehead, inflicting a bloody, nasty gash and a permanent scar that Jackson carried with him for the remainder of his life. Robert was not as lucky. The officer turned to him with the same command. When he similarly refused, the blade cut into his head, leaving a wound that helped end his life.

The British dispatched Andrew, Robert, and twenty other prisoners some forty miles to Camden. They found themselves in a dreadful camp with little food or clothing and no medical attention to their wounds. Smallpox ravaged the site, infecting both Jackson boys. Almost in time, Elizabeth persuaded a local partisan captain to trade his 13 British captives for seven Waxhaw Patriots. Robert was dying, the untreated wound, pox, and malnourishment leaving him unable to walk. He died at home several days later. An emaciated Andrew trekked back barefoot and in rags; somehow he hung on, surviving the pox and a fever that should have been fatal. The toughness and iron will that made Jackson legendary had revealed themselves.[3]

As her remaining son recovered, Elizabeth departed for Charleston to aid Crawford family members held in horrific conditions aboard a British prison ship in Charleston harbor. Andrew would never see her again. While providing her relatives with much-needed food and supplies, Elizabeth Jackson was struck by cholera and buried in an anonymous grave near the city. Her memory and admonitions both haunted and guided Jackson throughout his life. He remembered her counsel: making and keeping good friends was invaluable, and forgetting an obligation or being ungrateful for a kindness was "a base crime." Be polite, keep your self-esteem, and avoid quarrels, Elizabeth advised, but always sustain your manhood. Control your temper, and calmly defend your honor. Jackson embraced those tenets, if he did not always follow them. Undoubtedly, his mother was the major influence on his overall attitude toward life, prompting in particular a high regard for women. Only Rachel Donelson would rival Elizabeth in his affection.[4]

As one biographer emphasizes, "Andrew Jackson was now in a situation most perilous to a young man." He recovered at the home of relatives. At age fourteen, however, he lacked any immediate family or parental control, retaining a sense of honor and pride honed by the war to a razor's edge. Never particularly fond of his Latin and Greek studies, Jackson abandoned any pretense of pursuing his mother's clerical dream for a much-preferred, if temporary, life of dissipation. The boy was understandably depressed. He loved working at a relative's saddle shop, but the Waxhaws held memories of loss, death, and devastation.

Upon learning that he had inherited the equivalent of $40,000 from his grandfather in Scotland, Jackson made his way in December 1782 to vice-filled Charleston. The capital offered numerous venues to refine his gambling skills and to take a young man's money. Within weeks, he lost it all at drink, cards, cockfighting, horses, and, most easily, dice.

Seemingly without remorse, but with a new attitude that gave him purpose, Andrew returned to the Waxhaws. He had inherited the family farm and two hundred acres would provide a good income. Working behind a plow, however, had little appeal. He turned again to formal study, and even taught school. Yet the life of the mind seemed unrewarding, so Jackson decided to try his hand at the law. A career at the bar might actually suit him. He had the intelligence to comprehend the legal system and added even greater skills of verbal sparring and persuasion. Jackson knew the values and mindset of the frontiersman, and the courtroom, like the battlefield, allowed him to use his instincts.

With no traditional law school nearby, in December 1784, at age 17, Andrew traveled the 75 miles to Salisbury, North Carolina, to study with Spruce McCay. For the next two years he learned the rudiments of the profession, at least enough to pass the bar exam. Jackson was never one to let academics interfere with developing his social skills and advancing his position. Parties, dances, drinking, and gambling consumed a goodly amount of time in Salisbury, as he developed a reputation as a charismatic and ambitious young man of genuine promise. Although the presidential Jackson appears somewhat stiff and humorless, the teenage Jackson reveled in riotous behavior and practical jokes. When outhouses were moved, signs in the town disappeared, or tavern fights erupted, the locals knew in which direction to cast the blame. Jackson managed the Christmas ball for the community and invited two single women, Molly and Rachel Wood, to attend. This seemed a harmless, even a warm-hearted gesture given the season, but since the Woods were prostitutes, their appearance scandalized the town. Jackson had struck again.

After two years, he grew restless, departed Salisbury, and wandered about the region until the spring of 1788. The garrulous young lawyer made numerous friends, including John McNairy, elected as a judge in the western district of North Carolina—soon to become the state of Tennessee. McNairy offered his comrade steady work as a public prosecutor. With few real options, Jackson accepted a position that was high in risk and low in financial reward. Jackson and several friends rode west, but halted in Jonesborough for the summer when it became apparent that they could not arrive in Nashville for the commencement of the court session. First impressions mattered. Jackson moved with dispatch to establish his reputation as a gentleman and assert his honor. He purchased Nancy, a female slave approximately his own age, to demonstrate wealth and position. Slavery had assumed an irresistible foothold in Tennessee, and gained ground rapidly in the 1790s. Jackson, unlike some of his contemporaries in the early republic, was not conflicted about the moral or economic value of slavery. His upbringing and desire for material success encouraged a belief in black inferiority.[5]

Jackson's first duel resulted from an exchange of words in the courtroom with Waightstill Avery, a veteran lawyer whom Andrew had earlier sought out as a mentor in North Carolina. Circumstances at the time had dictated Avery's refusal to add the young Jackson as a student, but Andrew likely took the rebuff personally. When Avery insulted the sensitive Jackson publicly in the courtroom, a challenge was issued immediately. They wisely recognized, however, that the affront hardly merited risking their lives and the ensuing duel resulted in both men shooting their guns in the air. Honor had been served.[6]

In October 1788, Jackson made his way to Nashville, an area recently settled and lying in the heart of the Cumberland River Valley. The tightly knit village numbered only 200 people, but had a courthouse, businesses, and a distillery. Violence was all too present on the frontier. Pioneer John Donelson had been killed in 1785, perhaps by Indians or white outlaws. His widow, children, including daughter Rachel, and relatives remained among the most prominent citizens in the small community. Jackson and fellow lawyer John Overton desperately needed a place to stay, so they boarded with the Donelsons about 10 miles out of town. The family welcomed both the added income and two more guns in the event of an Indian attack.

Jackson could not help but notice the vivacious brown-haired, brown-eyed Rachel, a high-spirited beauty of his own age. Alluring and easy to talk to, she was among the best dancers and horsewomen in the county. Unfortunately, in 1785, Rachel had wed a wealthy Kentuckian, Lewis Robards. His jealousy, hot temper, and infidelities, however, put the marriage on a rocky path. Three years later, she fled Harrodsburgh to find refuge with her family in Nashville. This incident was only the first of a disastrous series of movements spanning the next two years, with both Rachel and Lewis travelling frequently between Kentucky and Tennessee in an effort to save their relationship.

Jackson no doubt observed the family drama play out in the Donelson household with considerable interest, but he had a career and reputation to build. Progress on the frontier meant expansion and the obstacles seemed numerous and powerful. The Indians proved a dogged enemy, especially for the new federal government under the Constitution, which lacked a significant army and evinced a lackluster commitment to removal of the Native Americans. The Spanish controlled Florida to the south, the Louisiana territory to the west, including New Orleans and the Mississippi River, a vital channel for commerce. In violation of the Peace of Paris treaties that ended the American Revolution, the English retained military and trading posts on U.S. soil, ranging from Vermont and New York into the Old Northwest of Ohio and Michigan. They also wisely remained concerned about the American desire for Canada.

Jackson firmly believed that the nation's destiny rested on the security of its borders, and, like Jefferson, on independent, white farmers tilling their own fields. Throughout his lifetime, Jackson constructed his career on fighting for them. Importantly, his vision for the country's future never included a place of power or influence for African Americans or Indians.

Accordingly, Jackson dedicated the next several years to intriguing in territorial politics and aligning himself with those individuals who could advance his national and personal ambitions. Andrew understood that boldness, courage, and instinct were valued much more than intellect in a frontier environment where danger and death lurked on the highway and in the forest. Loyalty mattered as well. In 1790, William Blount, a hard-charging land speculator whose family controlled over a million acres, had been appointed governor of the "Southwest Territory." Jackson found Blount his avenue to position and wealth. In turn, the governor knew he had encountered a talented and dedicated lawyer who would energetically pursue any task assigned him. Blount rewarded his young follower with the post of attorney general in 1791 and then, a year later, made him judge advocate in the Tennessee militia. In the 1790s, a combination of his legal practice and successful land ventures allowed Jackson the discretionary income to buy at least 16 slaves.

Within three years, the young barrister had already made his mark socially, economically, and politically. He was now prepared to claim the woman he believed should rightfully be his lifelong partner. Regrettably, Rachel Donelson Robards continued in a troubled and loveless match that offered no happy ending. Lewis remained perpetually jealous of his wife's flirtations, which may well have included Andrew Jackson. Robards' anger had gotten the best of him on several occasions, and heated words were exchanged as Jackson felt compelled to defend Rachel's honor. Although no duel resulted, Lewis threatened to whip Jackson, as the latter brandished a knife and offered to cut Robards's ears off.

In January 1790, when word reached Nashville that Robards wanted to reclaim his wife and take her back to Kentucky, Rachel fled, joining friends and family in Spanish-held Natchez along the Mississippi River. Jackson accompanied the small party, ostensibly for their protection. While Rachel stayed in Natchez, Andrew returned in May to handle his legal practice in Nashville, where he possibly heard in December that Robards had filed for divorce—on the grounds of his wife cohabiting with Jackson.

Divorce remained difficult to obtain in the early republic; justifications were few, favored the male, and required the permission of the state legislature. Andrew rushed back to Mississippi, where possibly he and Rachel wed in the spring of 1791, although no records exist to confirm the nuptials. They soon moved back to Nashville as a couple. Lamentably, Robards had only been given *permission* to sue for divorce by the Virginia legislature, which governed the Kentucky territory. The divorce itself would not be granted until the fall of 1793 and the Jacksons promptly married in January 1794. Consequently, Andrew and Rachel had lived in adultery for over two years. Historian Andrew Burstein persuasively argues that their morally shaky situation was not the product of innocence or "an honest mistake." The Jacksons knowingly took legal steps towards divorce when Rachel separated from Robards and moved to Natchez. In the 1828 presidential campaign, desertion and adultery became major issues as the entire nation, not just the frontier, applied middle-class values to the marriage. The love of Rachel and Andrew deepened over time, but society would not prove forgiving.[7]

Jackson had arrived in Nashville with little money, few friends, and no reputation. Now a prosperous attorney with a new bride and heightened connections, he joined the influential Masonic Order and purchased a plantation in 1796 at Hunter's Hill, some 13 miles from the city. Jackson farmed, traded slaves, and dabbled in mercantile ventures with various partners. His speculations often proved profitable, although he learned a painful lesson in 1795 when he journeyed to Philadelphia, the nation's capital, to sell almost 70,000 acres of land. David Allison bought the property for $13,750, but when Allison went bankrupt, his notes proved worthless. Jackson had spent the notes for his own purchases and now had to cover the losses. Although this experience put Jackson in debt for several years and taught him to be wary of paper money, he did not totally abandon its use. Nor did he stop speculating in land.[8]

With an eye towards increasing the wealth of whites of all classes, Andrew joined his fellow Tennesseans in demanding that the national government clear the land of the Indians. His prejudice against Native Americans was a product of his life experience. Indian cruelty and savagery were legendary in the Waxhaws, the threat proving all too real west of the Appalachians. In 1791–1792, Indians killed almost 100 white settlers in Jackson's judicial district and attacks unnerved small settlements like Nashville. As federal protection proved less than adequate, Jackson sought the status of statehood that would allow the residents to initiate their own more effective Indian policy.

Finally, in 1796, Tennesseans approved statehood, and the goal was achieved. Indian nemesis William Blount and Andrew Jackson would be appointed Tennessee's first U.S. Senator and Congressman respectively.

Andrew, who frequently travelled the territory on business matters, tried to convince Rachel of his contentment. "I mean to retire from the Buss of publick [sic] life," he asserted in May 1796, "and Spend My Time with you alone in Sweet Retirement, which is my only ambition and ultimate wish." His decision to accept the congressional post said otherwise. The pragmatic Blount brought no committed ideology with him to Philadelphia, easily moving from the Federalist to the Democratic Republican Party. The 29-year-old Jackson, however, already held firm expectations and beliefs. A fiscal conservative, he found the notion of federal taxation intrusive. Jackson likewise emphasized states' rights and favored limiting the government's constitutional authority in domestic matters.[9]

Conversely, he adopted a strongly nationalistic stance on defense and foreign policy, demanding that the government protect Americans both at home and abroad. He believed the administration of George Washington had disappointed in this regard, allowing Indians to run rampant on the frontier and the British to violate American rights by impressing sailors and seizing U.S. ships on the high seas. Jackson rejected the Jay Treaty with Great Britain of 1794 as a betrayal, since the agreement had not resolved these issues in America's favor. He did support Washington's and Adams's efforts, however, to build a new navy, and to defend the merchant marine against attack by the Barbary pirates in the Mediterranean Sea. Even so, the irritated congressman refused to endorse a House of Representatives' letter of thanks to Washington for his service. Jackson took umbrage at the departing president's famous Farewell Address to Congress, not only for its content, but he especially felt the speech smacked far too much of "monarchical expression"—like King George III addressing Parliament.

In March 1797, when the four-month session of Congress concluded, Jackson returned to Nashville with a sense of relief. Remaining active and vocal, the novice soon found the increasing partisanship of the capital distasteful. He enjoyed working with the majority Blount faction at home, but his Jeffersonian ideals were a minority position in Congress, subjecting him to ridicule by many in Federalist Philadelphia.[10]

A disenchanted Jackson attempted an alternate route to success, heightening his military profile by seeking the post of major general of the state militia. He lost that contest, but surprisingly found himself elected to the U.S. Senate. In 1797, the government discovered that William Blount was engaged in a conspiracy with the British to seize Florida and Louisiana from Spain. This revelation prompted the Senate to expel him that July, and his protégé was duly chosen by the Tennessee legislature to replace him. Jackson reluctantly journeyed back to the capital—the earlier trip had taken 42 days by horseback—for the November session with neither his wife to accompany him nor any political purpose to motivate him.

Andrew Jackson served less than a year combined in the House and Senate. Clearly, the role of a legislator was not his strength. An adequate speaker, the planter was, however, no orator. One source recalled that his voice was strong and penetrating and that he revealed a theatrical flair for waving his arms above his head and pointing with his forefinger for effectiveness. "No one ever listened to a speech or a talk from Andrew Jackson who, when he was done, had the least doubt as to what he was driving at."

Yet, Jackson rarely spoke in Congress. His limited agenda focused on protecting the frontier and promoting the national defense. His views on foreign affairs reflected a predictably anti-English bias; hence he cheered on Napoleon Bonaparte in France's war with Great Britain. "Should Bonaparte make a landing on the English shore," he assured a friend, "tyranny will be humbled, a throne crushed and a republic will spring from the wreck—and millions of distressed people restore to the rights of man." As a backwoodsman, lacking in formal education, worldly travel, and rhetorical skills, Jackson's growing discomfort, especially in a small body such as the Senate, must have been troubling.[11]

He made a few friends in Congress, mostly notably future Secretary of the Treasury Albert Gallatin, but never became adept at playing politics. Jackson deeply resented the patronage policies that threw perfectly qualified men out of their jobs for partisan reasons. Perhaps not surprisingly, he also failed to bond with party leader and Vice President Thomas Jefferson. Jackson, of course, aspired to become a frontier aristocrat, sharing the "Sage of Monticello's" support of the white yeoman farmer, slavery, a belief in the virtue of the agrarian lifestyle, and a reverence for states rights' principles. Jackson might also respect the Virginian's intellectual prowess, but a conversation between the erudite scholar of the Enlightenment and the rough-hewn, sometimes impetuous, man of action may well have been brief. Someone who gambled, drank, took risks, behaved violently, and held honor and family sacred was to be admired on the frontier. How could Jackson really venerate a gentleman who never fought a duel? For his part, Jefferson remained cordial to Jackson, but never identified with his mercurial temper and military pretensions.

Although skilled in various social surroundings and an admirer of the ladies, Jackson was unsuccessful in establishing his public footing in Philadelphia. At thirty, he remained charming, even dashing, but he undoubtedly felt empty and alone without Rachel by his side—"my love" as he addressed her in their correspondence. He struggled with guilt, knowing his wife endured loneliness and depression and resented his absence. The decision to resign his Senate seat in April 1798 after only one unrewarding session was not difficult.[12]

He welcomed the chance to reclaim his place in Nashville society and recover financially from the disastrous Allison affair. In December, election as a state Superior Court judge at $600 a year helped provide a foundation. Concurrently, Jackson advanced his commercial and plantation interests, including partnering in a general store and distillery and employing the first cotton gin in the Cumberland Valley.

Jackson served on the bench for six years. Although far from learned in the law, he could be counted on to render his decisions with energy and fairness. Eventually, the judiciary proved unsatisfying, both from a financial and personal vantage point. The military held greater promise of advancement and reward. Service in the state militia rarely involved combat. Usually, the meetings offered local males the opportunity to socialize and bond over bottomless glasses of whiskey. The situation, of course, differed somewhat in Tennessee where the Indians remained a threat for the next several decades. Even when their resistance was crushed in the War of 1812, they continued to occupy lands coveted by white farmers. Jackson recognized that he might propel his army career by broadening his circle of associates and demonstrating his leadership skills in battle against the natives. Consequently, he challenged former Governor John Sevier for the elected post of major general.

The two men shared a tenuous relationship reaching back a decade to Jackson's political alliance with William Blount. While Sevier and Blount battled for power, Andrew made his loyalties clear. Those loyalties had been rewarded. When Blount died in 1800, Jackson emerged as a leader of their west Tennessee faction. A Sevier-Jackson confrontation appeared inevitable. Bad blood surfaced in 1802 when Jackson, with the support of Governor Archibald Roane, narrowly defeated Sevier for the major-generalship. Jackson perhaps repaid his debt to Roane by revealing information during the 1803 gubernatorial campaign indicating that Sevier had been involved in speculation and land fraud.

The charge irritated Sevier more than it did the Tennessee voters, who returned the former governor to office. When Jackson and Sevier encountered each other in Knoxville in early October, heated words were exchanged relating to each man's contributions to the state. An exasperated Sevier purportedly snarled at Jackson that "the only service he had performed is taking another man's wife in Natchez." A furious Andrew responded, "Great God! Do you mention *her* sacred name?" Shots were fired without damage, but Jackson could not let the insult pass. The next day he published a letter branding Sevier "a base coward and poltroon" and challenging him to a duel. The governor and the general arranged a contest that never took place. Sevier failed to appear at the agreed dueling location, though the two parties met again on the road outside of Knoxville. Once more, insults were hurled, pistols and swords drawn. Thankfully, no shots were fired, nor was anyone harmed. Jackson was unable to salve his honor or gain the satisfaction he wanted. Worse still, he damaged his own reputation and influence by further alienating Sevier, who remained governor until 1808 as well as commander of the militia forces in east Tennessee.[13]

Lighting the fuse of Jackson's pride required a very small match. The matter of his controversial courtship of Rachel, and of their ensuing marriage and re-marriage, provided fuel for gossip, rumor, and insult throughout their lives. In the small towns and villages of the frontier, pre-marital sex and the often resultant pregnancies were somewhat commonplace, if not fully accepted, aspects of a society that was grounded in evangelical Protestant faith and a code of honor. Rachel's transgression related, however, to her perceived infidelity as a married woman. Once virtue was sacrificed, it was almost impossible to reclaim. The Jacksons became targets for social exclusion from a large segment of "respectable" Nashville society.

An escape to a new plantation and economic prosperity helped heal some of their wounds. Andrew sold the farm at Hunter's Hill, moving to a 420-acre plot outside the city, the land that would house the classically styled and elegant "Hermitage." He abandoned not only his judgeship, but also his legal practice altogether, turning successfully to cotton growing, land speculation, and burgeoning mercantile interests. As more labor was needed to work the fields, by the 1830s Jackson had dramatically increased his work force to 150 slaves. He could indeed be a kind, even generous, master. As with all individuals under his command, however, he had little patience for disobedience. Hardworking, obedient slaves were rewarded for their behavior. In his absence, Rachel was mistress of the Hermitage, but the property and slaves were supervised daily by overseer Benjamin Person. Jackson was comfortable that Person would do Rachel's bidding, instructing her in late 1823, "I do not wish my hands labored too hard—&if [sic] you think they are, I know when you name it to him he will moderate— I wish them well fed, & warmly clothed and they will be then contented and happy. This is my wish—I do not want them in any way oppressed and if they behave well I am sure Mr. Parsons [sic] knowing my wishes will treat them well."

In 1829, Jackson suspected another overseer, Graves Steele, of mistreating his slaves, perhaps resulting in the death of Jack and Jim, two of the president's "family." An angry Jackson reminded his son that Steele had been told, "My negroes shall be treated humanely . . . feed and clothe them well, and work them in moderation. If he has deviated from this rule, he must be discharged." Incensed by further information regarding Steele's cruelty, Jackson fumed, "I cannot bear the inhumanity that he has exercised towards my poor negroes, contrary to his promise."

On the other hand, Jackson could order the whip when deemed necessary. As he directed Egbert Harris at his plantation in Big Springs, Alabama, "As far as leniency can be extended to these unfortunate creatures, I wish you to do so; subordination must be obtained first, and then good treatment." Running away and insolent behavior particularly irritated him. When a mulatto male ran in 1804, Jackson placed an advertisement in the newspaper offering a $50 reward for his capture—and an added $10 if one hundred lashes were administered as punishment. In 1822, a slave named Gilbert escaped. An exasperated Jackson commanded that after recapture he should be "sold down the river." Instead, Gilbert spent several years at the Hermitage where in 1824 and 1827 he ran away again. The last attempt resulted in a confrontation in which overseer Ira Walton killed Gilbert for resisting a whipping.

Women were not immune from punishment. Jackson ran out of patience with Betty, a slave of about 30 at the Hermitage. Away in Florida in the summer of 1821, he ordered that his manager "severely chastised [her] on the first imprudent or improper conduct" by administering fifty lashes.[14]

Through the shifting and uneven economic landscape, Jackson maintained his appetite for gambling, especially cockfighting and horseracing, a passion that would once again cripple his reputation and almost cost his life. In 1805, Jackson invested $1,500 in Truxton, a five-year-old Virginia bay of unparalleled speed. Truxton's success allowed Jackson to expand his stable, and also resulted in a challenge from rival horse owner Joseph Erwin. Erwin's Ploughboy would race Truxton in late November for $2,000—a sizeable purse. When a lame Ploughboy withdrew from the contest, Erwin and his son-in-law, Charles Dickinson, were obliged to pay an agreed upon $800 as the forfeit fee. The sum was to be disbursed in various promissory notes, the nature of those notes becoming the subject of discussion between Erwin and Jackson. Apparently, Dickinson entered the conversation and besmirched Rachel's name, something sure to get Jackson's blood boiling. Over the course of the next several months, the situation became increasingly confused as to whether various people involved in the matter had misrepresented the truth—or lied. Jackson and Dickinson, a 26-year-old attorney and expert marksman, exchanged insults. The language spiraled out of control with "worthless," "scoundrel," "poltroon," and "coward" liberally used. A needless duel could not be far behind.

On the cool Kentucky morning of May 30, 1806, the two men faced each other at a distance of twenty-four feet with pistols raised. Dickinson, confident to the point of arrogance, joined the local betting pool, wagering $300 that he would kill Jackson. He fired first, his ball striking Jackson in the chest near the heart. Somehow Jackson remained standing, as a dumbfounded Dickinson looked on in amazement. When Jackson pulled the trigger, the pistol failed to discharge, but a reset and second effort sent Dickinson tumbling to the ground with a bullet lodged in his abdomen. He died within the day. Meanwhile, Jackson made his way home, the lead remaining in his breast for the remainder of his life.

Although Jackson survived, his reputation suffered a near-death experience as a result of killing his popular young adversary. Some Tennesseans charged Jackson with murder—that he need not have reset and fired his weapon. Honor had been satisfied. Jackson disagreed, and paid a price in further social isolation. With his pride assuaged and Rachel's virtue defended, he returned to his business interests at the Hermitage.[15]

In spite of the setbacks with Sevier, Jackson remained engaged in state and national politics, especially as it might advance his own interests or those of the United States. In 1804, Tennessee's congressional delegation had submitted his name to Thomas Jefferson as the governor of the Territory of Orleans. Jackson coveted the post, but the president was informed that the passionate Tennessean would be unsuitable. Jefferson never seriously considered the volatile Jackson, and selected the more diplomatic and conciliatory William C. Claiborne.

No doubt, Jackson's disenchantment with the White House grew with the rejection. To Andrew, the well-intentioned Jefferson had strayed from the ideological path that brought Jackson in line with the Democratic-Republican Party in the 1790s. As president, the Virginian inadequately defended the national honor of the United States against insults from both Great Britain and Spain. Ongoing British seizures of American ships and cargoes on the high seas and the impressment of sailors into His Majesty's navy had been met with a timid and ineffective economic response from Jefferson and Secretary of State James Madison. Similarly, the Spanish, who still controlled Florida, Texas, and the Southwest, remained an obstacle to U.S. expansion. They eagerly conspired with anyone willing to thwart American settlement to the West.

During 1805–1806, when former Vice President Aaron Burr organized his ill-fated intrigue to invade Spanish-held territories in the Southwest, an eager Jackson assisted with obtaining provisions and ships. Ever the expansionist and defender of American security, Jackson assumed that the plan, which might involve conquering parts of Florida, Texas, and even Mexico, had tacit White House approval. Discovering that the material and political interests of the conspirators and not the nation were foremost, Jackson abruptly backed off, informing Jefferson of the scheme and agreeing in 1807 to testify at Burr's trial in Richmond. Jackson defended the patriotic intent of the original plan. He laid the blame for the deviation not on Burr, but on his accomplice, General James Wilkinson, a man Jackson genuinely despised. Wilkinson, as the commanding general in the West, had ended the military career of Jackson's close friend, Thomas Butler, over whether

Butler, a Revolutionary War veteran, could wear his hair in a long queue—in violation of a new army mandate.[16]

Ultimately, Jackson was never called as a witness at the Burr trial. Burr was found not guilty, and Wilkinson improbably escaped indictment despite the best efforts of a grand jury to link him with the plot. Jackson became disillusioned, but remained defiant. When war with Spain seemed imminent in the winter of 1806, the president called out the state militia. An excited Jackson confided his long-held views to Governor Claiborne, "I love my country and Government, I hate the Dons—I would delight to see Mexico reduced, but I will die in the last ditch before I would yield a part to the Dons, or see the Union disunited." As the crisis quickly passed, however, and the government ordered Jackson to dismiss his men, the disappointed general muttered to a compatriot that Secretary of War Henry Dearborn was "not fit for a Grany [sic]."[17]

By 1810, Jackson seemed at the end of his career as a public man. He still maintained his post as major general of the militia, preparing himself and his men for the call to crush the Indians or Spanish. That call never seemed to come. Angered and frustrated by Jefferson's reluctance to appoint him to office and by the administration's futile policies, Jackson had thrown his support to James Monroe against James Madison in 1808 for the party's presidential nomination. Monroe, an avowed states' rights supporter, failed in his challenge, and Madison cruised to victory in the fall election over his Federalist rival Charles Cotesworth Pinckney. Jackson's fading national profile was complemented in Tennessee by his alienation from Sevier and local criticism resulting from the Dickinson duel.

The situation in Nashville further disintegrated in March 1807 when Andrew engaged in a scuffle in the street with business partner Samuel Jackson. The exchange, involving a dispute over debts, resulted in Samuel throwing a rock at Andrew's head (he missed) and Andrew in response plunged his sword cane thorough Samuel's coat (he also missed.) Fisticuffs followed that did credit to neither man before bystanders broke up the fight. Samuel filed charges, but a jury acquitted Andrew of assault. Even so, local residents were left to wonder about Jackson's temper, penchant for violence, and perhaps his mental stability.

From his own vantage point, Jackson had worked hard over the past two decades. His labors enhanced the personal fortunes of his family, enlarged in 1809 with the adoption of his infant nephew, Andrew, Jr. However, at age forty-three, his exaggerated sense of honor, pride, and willful nature had severely damaged his reputation. He had compiled an impressive list of enemies, or at least those who were unlikely to promote his career, including Jefferson, Madison, Wilkinson, and Sevier. It seemed improbable that history would again record the name of Andrew Jackson.[18]

Notes

1. Robert V. Remini, *Andrew Jackson and the Course of American Empire, 1767–1821* (New York: Harper and Row, 1977), 30–31.
2. Marquis James, *The Life of Andrew Jackson* (New York: Bobbs–Merrill, 1938), 3–11.
3. "Jackson's Description of His Experiences," Sam B. Smith and Harriet Chappell Owsley, eds., *The Papers of Andrew Jackson,* I, (Knoxville: University of Tennessee Press, 1980), 5–7. Hereafter cited as the *Jackson Papers.* Amos Kendall, *The Life of Andrew Jackson* (1843), 13.
4. H.W. Brands, *Andrew Jackson: His Life and Times* (New York: Anchor Books, 2006), 31.
5. Record of Slave Sale, November 17, 1788, *Jackson Papers,* I, 15.
6. Jackson, August 12, 1788, to Waightstill Avery, *Jackson Papers,* I, 12.
7. Andrew Burstein, *The Passions of Andrew Jackson* (New York: A.A. Knopf, 2003), 240–248; Mark R. Cheathem, *Andrew Jackson: Southerner* (Baton Rouge: Louisiana State University Press, 2013), 20–23.
8. Agreement with David Allison, May 14, 1795, *Jackson Papers,* I, 56–57.
9. Jackson, May 9, 1796, to Rachel, *Jackson Papers,* I, 91–92.
10. Cheathem, *Southerner,* 26, 32–36; Brands, *Andrew Jackson,* 80.
11. Jackson, January 11, 1798, to James Robertson, *Jackson Papers,* I, 164–65.
12. A.C. Buell, *History of Andrew Jackson (*New York: Charles Scribner's Sons, 1904), I, 111–25.
13. Jackson, October 10, 1803, to J. Sevier, *Jackson Papers,* I, 378–79*;* J. Sevier, October 10, 1803, to Jackson, ibid. 380–81; Cheathem, *Southerner,* 39–41.
14. Runaway Ad, September 26, 1804, *Jackson Papers,* II, 41; Jackson, December 11, 1823, to Rachel, ibid., V, 324–25; Jackson, July 4, 1829, to Andrew Jackson, Jr., ibid., VII, XXXX; Jackson, April 13, 1822, to Egbert Harris, ibid, V, 170–71; Jackson, July 3, 1821, to James C. Bronough, ibid., 66–67.
15. Burstein, *Passions,* 51–61; Cheathem, *Southerner,* 41–45.
16. Burstein, *Passions,* 68–84; Jackson, August 3, 1804, to T. Jefferson, *Jackson Papers,* II, 33–35.
17. Cheathem, *Southerner,* 46–48; Jackson, November 12, 1806, to WCC Claiborne, *Jackson Papers,* II, 116; Jackson, November 28, 1807, to Daniel Smith, ibid., 174–76; Jackson, February 10, 1810, to John Randolph, ibid., 234–35; Jackson, October 4, 1806, to James Winchester, ibid., 110–11; Jackson, January 3, 1807, to William P. Anderson, ibid., 134.
18. Court Minutes in State v. Andrew Jackson, November 9, 1807, *Jackson Papers,* II, 172–74; Dumas Malone, *Jefferson the President: First Term, 1801–1805* (Boston: Little, Brown, 1970), 357–58.

CHAPTER 2

THE BORDER CAPTAIN

BRITISH AND INDIAN THREATS (1812–1818)

The drums of war beat loudly in 1812. From New York to New Orleans, the rising tide of anger over continued British affronts to American honor and commercial violations on the high seas placed the Madison administration—poised for reelection in November—in a difficult situation. New England, a Federalist stronghold and the heartbeat of U.S. shipping, strongly opposed a conflict with Great Britain that would jeopardize trade and profits. In the West and South, however, "War Hawks" clamored for a defense of the republic, not just as a matter of honor, but also as a vehicle to seize British-held Canada and Spanish colonial Florida. The Indians in the Old Northwest and Southwest, especially the Shawnee and Creek, aided by their European allies, had been more than troublesome. With London deeply embroiled in the Napoleonic Wars and awaiting the outcome of the "Little Corporal's" invasion of Russia, and Spain torn apart by civil war and the rising tide of revolution in her South American possessions, many Democratic-Republicans determined the time was ripe for American action.

The president's request for a declaration of war rested primarily on relentless and offensive British policies. His statement met with the overwhelming approval of his party, and a similar rejection from the opposition Federalists. On June 17, 1812, the Senate, reflecting the divided nation, voted for war by a narrow margin. For Andrew Jackson, the administration had finally asserted itself in defense of the flag and for American expansion.

He still held his commission as major general, but would wait months for the call to arms. The memory of his involvement with Burr's conspiracy and opposition to Madison's nomination in 1808 still lingered in Washington. Meanwhile, the southern frontier remained exposed to attack from both the Indians in Alabama and the Royal Navy along the Gulf Coast.

Jackson, convinced that the Creeks were "urged on by British agents and tools," declared, "*They must be punished*—and our frontier protected." The general impatiently languished in Nashville, before finally receiving orders in October to raise a body of Tennessee volunteers for the defense of New Orleans and the lower Mississippi River. He confided his only fear to good friend George Washington Campbell, "Should we be ordered to Join Genl. Wilkeson [sic], he is so universally disliked by our citizens that something unpleasant may arise . . . It is a bitter pill to have to act with him, but for my countries good I will swallow it." Bad luck prevailed and Jackson found himself and his 2,000 soldiers under Wilkinson's command. Fortunately, the two old enemies put their personal issues aside, and cautiously cooperated in January 1813, as the Tennessee regiments moved towards Natchez. Perhaps both men realized that the timely arrival of Jackson's men would be the salvation of New Orleans. Much to Jackson's disgust, however, he received word in March from the War Department to halt his advance and immediately dismiss his troops. The perceived threat along the Mississippi River had evaporated.[1]

Rachel Jackson took comfort at the news. Emotionally weary and depressed, she implored, "Do not My beloved Husband let the love of Country fame and honour [sic] make you forgit [sic] you have me . . . how many pangs how many heart rendings Sighs has your absence Cost me." She also soon discovered that when the New Orleans mission had been curtailed by the government, Andrew had written a letter to his friend William B. Lewis (and also Secretary of War John Armstrong) expressing a desire to be "ordered to upper Canedy [sic]." "How can you wish such a perilous tower but the Love of Country the thirst for Honour [sic] and patriotism is your motive," Rachel chided. Jackson responded to his wife with bitterness about the callous disregard for his men—abandoned by the War Department, sick and without supplies, 800 miles from home. The resolute commander determined to remain with his soldiers until their plight was resolved. He would march them home. Andrew assured Rachel that he would be with her "shortly."

When he did arrive in Nashville in April, Jackson promptly rebuked Secretary Armstrong for not dispatching his well-disciplined Tennesseans to the Detroit frontier. No doubt Rachel was correct about both her husband's patriotism and his ambition. The aborted New Orleans campaign failed to reveal if Jackson could transfer his courage on the dueling ground to the battlefield, but certainly he had demonstrated skills of command, leadership, training, and organization. He had the respect of his men; they rewarded his toughness by branding him "Old Hickory."[2]

The year 1812 had been disastrous for American forces all along the Canadian frontier. Washington prepared to launch more invigorated initiatives in 1813, but the administration seemed resolved to disregard Jackson's talents. They tapped William Henry Harrison, Wade Hampton, and even James Wilkinson to lead armies in the summer campaigns. Fuming, Jackson waited again. He had recently mentored a number of junior officers, including 31-year-old North Carolina lawyer Thomas Hart Benton. Benton hoped to advance his career in the capital, where he reported in June that friendly and appreciative individuals were lobbying for a brigadier-generalship for Jackson and a possible command. Nothing seemed definite, and Jackson was indeed ignored. As he contemplated his future, personal relationships once again threatened his reputation. Another of his young officers, William Carroll, combatted Benton's brother Jesse in a duel with Jackson acting as his second. The resulting comedic exchange of fire at only 10 feet left Carroll with a wounded thumb, and Jesse Benton with a grazed posterior. The humiliated Jesse became the butt of jokes for years in Nashville, a situation his brother sought to remedy.

Thomas believed that Jackson, older, wiser, and more experienced in the *code duello*, should have acted as a peacemaker between the two novices. Jackson had, in fact, attempted to negotiate the dispute to an amicable settlement, but words and deeds spiraled out of his control. Ensuing written exchanges and public rumors seemed to impugn Jackson's honor and judgment. A clash was inevitable. In September, when the two men encountered each other in Nashville at the City Hotel, a melee ensued that once again almost ended Jackson's life. Jackson brandished his whip and threatened Thomas, who attempted to pull a gun in his defense. Old Hickory drew his own pistol and backed Thomas through the hotel door, where a lurking Jesse fired into Jackson. The two shots hit Jackson in the left arm and shoulder dropping him to the floor. Jackson's compatriots outside the hotel rushed to his rescue. Somehow, in the resultant brawl with swords, daggers, and pistols, no one died.

As doctors tried to stop the gushing flow of blood, however, Jackson soaked through two mattresses. Defying pleas from the physicians to amputate, he defiantly vowed to keep his arm, and the bullet remained in the limb for the next 20 years. Weakened by the loss of blood, Jackson stayed in bed at the Nashville Inn for the next three weeks. Once again, he survived an almost fatal confrontation that many would have deemed needless. This time, however, the manner of the attack discredited the Bentons, not Andrew Jackson. Once a friend and disciple of the general, Thomas felt compelled to move west to redeem himself and his reputation. Within a decade, Benton was elected to the U.S. Senate from Missouri, and soon became one of Jackson's most trusted allies and supporters in Congress.[3]

While Jackson recovered from his wounds, civil war erupted in Alabama among the Indians, a conflict that would bring him back into prominence. Among the most numerous and dangerous tribes, the Creeks, numbering

20,000, were divided between "upper" and "lower" factions. They either broadly resented and resisted the seizure of their land and destruction of their culture by invasive white farmers, or sought accommodation or perhaps even assimilation with whites as a reasonable course of action. In 1812, these differences erupted in violence between the two groups which spilled over to involve settlers on the frontier. On August 30, 1813, near Mobile, Alabama, a thousand upper Creek "Red Sticks" overran a stockade named Fort Mims and slaughtered some 250 white men, women, and children. The nature of the massacre of innocents spread quickly across Tennessee and the demand for Andrew Jackson to take command rose to a crescendo. Had he not warned of the Indian menace aided by their Spanish and British allies? Assembling his force of 2,500 in west Tennessee in early October, Jackson was ordered, along with several other American armies, to advance into Alabama territory and destroy the hostile Indians. They succeeded.

Over the next six months Jackson's men burned villages and crops, and contested the Red Sticks in a series of battles that became massacres. In late March 1814, the power of the mighty Creeks was finally broken at Horseshoe Bend, where the Indians lost 900 warriors. Throughout the lengthy campaign, Jackson, suffering from dysentery, and with a useless left arm dangling by his side, had to battle not only the enemy, but his own disgruntled soldiers. Literally starving and with little medical care, their enlistment time in the army expiring, the troops demanded to go home. Deserters departed quietly, while the mutineers challenged authority. Their commander appealed first to their patriotism, and when that failed, defiantly sat astride his horse, "The Duke," in front of his men and threatened to shoot anyone who quit the campaign. That more direct appeal succeeded. As Jackson asserted to Rachel, "you know my motto, I know you approve of it—that is death before dishonor." The general felt no shame as his men trudged back to Nashville in April 1814, where they were hailed as conquering heroes.

The War of 1812 offered little for Americans to celebrate, but Jackson's resounding triumph over the Creeks compelled even his old enemies in Washington to recognize his talents. In a conflict sorely lacking in charismatic leadership and battlefield success, Jackson demonstrated the ability to organize and lead his raw army to victory and help secure the southern frontier. Colonel Winfield Scott, later to become a hero of the Mexican War of 1846, observed that the veteran commanders in 1812 "had very generally slunk into sloth, ignorance, or habits of intemperate drinking." Indeed, that descriptor did not fit Jackson or William Henry Harrison, who received similar praise for his feats in the Northwest. Harrison first attacked the Indians at Tippecanoe in 1811, claiming a rather dubious victory over forces loyal to the Shawnee chieftain Tecumseh. He then pursued the

Indians and their British allies into Canada in October 1813, resulting in Tecumseh's death and a U.S. victory at the Battle of the Thames. Ironically, it was those triumphs achieved in the South and West, not the ill-fated invasions of eastern Canada, that would help catapult the two frontier generals into the White House.[4]

Certainly, Jackson's prolonged six-month absence from the Hermitage had tormented Rachel, who desperately missed his companionship and feared for his fragile health. His description of the carnage disturbed her deeply. She wanted her "dearest life" to come home, and reassured him, "You have served your Country Long Enough, you have gained maney Larells you have Ernd them." Jackson would not abandon a campaign half-concluded, but he did the unpredictable. He sent an Indian boy named Theodore to the Hermitage to alleviate Rachel's loneliness. Tragically, the child died in early 1814. Soon after, fate intervened. A ten-month-old infant, orphaned at the Battle of Tallushatchee in November 1813, was brought to Jackson's tent. When the Creek women of the village refused to care for the child, Jackson decided to send him back to Nashville. His motive is unclear, but Jackson certainly wanted the boy to "be one of our family," and was concerned about how little Andrew would respond to another son in the household.

A psychologist might suggest that the general was thinking of a way to cheer his distraught wife by placing an infant in her care, or perhaps he sought a playmate for Andrew. No doubt, Old Hickory felt compassion for a boy who found himself alone, like the youthful Jackson, without family. He indicated as much in a letter to Rachel reflecting upon "Lyncoya's" orphan status. Whatever the reason, the child was raised at the Hermitage, although historians differ as to the equality of his treatment within the family. Sympathetic biographer Robert Remini argues that Andrew and Rachel loved Lyncoya and the boy received "almost every advantage a planter's son enjoyed." Jackson's letters appear to tell a somewhat different story regarding emotional bonding. In 1814, the general invariably admonished his wife "to kiss my little Andrew for me," and inquired about his health and education. He also expressed concern for Lyncoya, but the paternal attachment seems missing. Remini concedes that the boy remained attached to his Creek roots and did run away several times. In 1817, the Jacksons adopted another relative, six-year-old Andrew Jackson Hutchings. Jackson instructed Rachel to "kiss my two little fellows for me, and tell them papa is well" and "kiss my two little Andrews for me." There was no mention of of Lyncoya.[5]

Lyncoya's presence in the Jackson household (he did refer to the boy as his "son"), also offers insight into Old Hickory's broader view of native peoples. He did not hate or want to kill all Indians. Like many Americans, including Thomas Jefferson, he viewed them as an obstacle to civilization as represented by the progress of white farmers, and as a threat to the security of the nation. They were undeniably in a savage state, but not inherently ignorant or evil. Jackson's approach then was paternalistic, not genocidal. He could coldly tell Rachel about slaughtering Indians in battle—"It was dark before we finished killing them"—and just as easily show compassion. "It is enough to make Humanity shudder to see the distressed situation of the Indians, Eight thousand are kept alive, being fed by the Government daily," he confided. "Could you only see the misery and wretchedness of those creatures perishing from want of food and picking up the grains of corn scattered from the mouths of horses and trodden in the earth—I know your humanity would feel for them." Jackson described Indians as "his children," and labored to separate the "good" Indians—those who would assimilate and become "civilized" by adopting an agrarian white lifestyle and Anglo laws—and "bad" Indians—those who retained the old ways roaming the land, and rejecting the future. Jackson sought out and benefited from the assistance he received on numerous campaigns from "friendly" Indians— "his brothers." When loyal Chehaw warriors joined the Americans during the Seminole expedition of 1818, about 270 Georgia militia raided their village, massacring the women and children left behind. Jackson, furious at the outrage and its impact on the loyalty of the Chehaw, penned a scathing letter to Governor William Rabun of Georgia blasting the "base, cowardly, and inhuman attack" which Jackson promised would "to the last ages fix a stain upon the character of Georgia." He demanded the arrest and punishment of the militia commander, who ultimately managed to escape imprisonment and make his way to safety in Havana.

The general's rather mixed respect for the Indian did not extend to recognizing them as independent nations, and the federal government helped no one by negotiating treaties that encouraged independence and discouraged accommodation. While never advocating Indian equality, Jackson believed that they could, and perhaps should, retain their cultural and racial identity, and live productive lives separate from whites across the Mississippi River.[6]

Over the summer of 1814, Jackson busied himself with the very important task of resolving the land issues with the defeated Indians. "Sharp Knife," as the Creeks labeled him, exacted harsh terms. The Treaty of Fort Jackson, signed on August 9, compelled the surrender of almost half their tribal lands in Alabama and Georgia. For Jackson, eliminating the Indian threat along the frontier and obtaining their land for white farmers was only half the battle. The border would never be secure until the U.S. convinced the Europeans to stop meddling in American affairs. Specifically, the British must be discouraged from aiding and abetting Indian resistance and the Spanish, who harbored the Seminoles and runaway slaves, removed from the Floridas. Jackson and Harrison had taken the initial steps towards splintering any alliance through their victories over the Creeks and Tecumseh's confederacy. The Americans must continue to press their advantage.

The turn of events in Europe, however, dramatically challenged any furthering of U.S. goals in 1814. A British-led coalition of allied nations defeated Napoleon, forced his abdication in April, and sent him into exile on the island of Elba in the Mediterranean. This triumph freed both the Royal army and navy to aggressively pursue the war against the United States. His Majesty's government dispatched an army of 10,000 veterans to Quebec to prepare for an invasion of the Northeast. Concurrently, the English navy also began its lethal attack on the coastline from Maine to Maryland. The fleet successfully sacked and burned towns along the Atlantic, including Washington, DC, until late August when they reached Baltimore. There, with bombs bursting in air, the defenders of Fort McHenry withstood the British onslaught and became immortalized by Francis Scott Key. The British forces in Canada enjoyed less success, and were forced to retreat when the Americans defeated them in mid-September at Plattsburgh, New York on Lake Champlain. The Crown had already planned to attack the vulnerable Gulf coast, and with the setbacks in the late summer, shifted its attention to seizing Mobile and New Orleans. Jackson would be waiting.

In early August, Jackson, now a major general commanding the Seventh Military District, received his orders to proceed to Mobile to defend the Gulf coast. He had just concluded his negotiations with the Creeks, and hoped to reunite with Rachel at the Hermitage. "Fortune that fickle dame, mars all my wishes," he told her. Jackson had accepted the responsibility of command, and assured Rachel, "my honor never shall be stained." He owed the British "a debt of retaliatory vengeance" and longed to pay off that debt on the battlefield. By August 22, Old Hickory and his 4,000 soldiers reached Mobile. Spain had abandoned all pretense of neutrality, allowing British forces to utilize Pensacola as a base for their assault. The broader plan involved the seizure of Louisiana and the lower Mississippi River, thus halting any westward movement of American settlers and protecting Indian lands. Jackson anticipated correctly; the British did launch an assault on September 15, but the combined land-sea attack was turned back at Fort Bowyer, south of Mobile. Since that tactic failed, the English reconsidered their next move.

Meanwhile, Jackson decided to root out the evil at its base by seizing Pensacola. However, the U.S. was not at war with Spain and the general lacked approval from the War Department to violate Florida's borders. No matter. Within two days of his arrival in Mobile, Jackson dispatched a letter advising Governor Mateo Gonzalez Manrique in Pensacola that he was aware of the Spanish providing rations to the Creeks ("refugee banditti") and British officers offering them military advice. Spain must "restrain the

Tomahawk and Scalping knife," or there would be consequences. Jackson promised "An Eye for an Eye, Toothe for Toothe, and Scalp for Scalp." Learning that the British had landed hundreds of troops with large quantities of arms and ammunition at the harbor, he could no longer wait for authorization from Washington.

In an October letter to new Secretary of War James Monroe, Jackson easily rationalized a strike on Pensacola. An end to the nascent British campaign against Mobile and New Orleans and a satisfactory defense of the Union could only be achieved by driving the country's enemies out of their Florida base. He was well aware that he risked censure by the administration and the loss of his commission, if not court-martial, for his actions. In Washington, the government nervously awaited the outcome of the unfolding drama. Fear of rupturing relations with Madrid prompted a cautious posture. Officials were reluctant to grant their bold general the formal approval he desired, but they secretly entertained hopes for his success.[7]

With lightning speed, the attack took place on November 7, 1814. The Americans and their Choctaw Indian allies stormed and occupied the city so rapidly that the accompanying firing resulted in few casualties on either side. The British fleet, with red-coated troops aboard, abandoned the Spanish to their fate. Governor Gonzalez Manrique surrendered his town, but Jackson had no interest in remaining. Fort Barrancas, which defended Pensacola, had been destroyed. Since the city offered an excellent harbor, but no particular resources, ongoing occupation was pointless. With the Spanish cowed and the British gone, Jackson had made his point. He returned to Alabama and even greater applause from appreciative westerners. The cooperative ties between Spain and Great Britain were now frayed beyond repair. Hostile Indians remained, however, and continued to pose an unsolved border problem that would require future resolution. The general only briefly basked in his success. Word arrived that the British were about to invade Louisiana.[8]

Jackson arrived in New Orleans on December 1, a gaunt figure seemingly in no condition to lead an army. His health deteriorating, he called for the aid and comfort of "his dearest love." Rachel would not arrive until mid-March 1815. However, in the interim, her husband became a national hero. Jackson had risen to the occasion to smite his boyhood enemy. He first cemented relations with the "Crescent City" community, charming the ladies and impressing the men with his bearing and character. New Orleans would not fall. Facing a powerful British fleet and a 6,000-man army, Jackson energetically began recruiting. He relied on his Kentucky and Tennessee troops and the local and state militia, but accepted almost anyone who could carry a musket, including free African Americans and local pirates led by the notorious Jean Lafitte. The loyal Choctaws would scout the swamps.[9]

The British landed in mid-December, launching a series of skirmishes that edged the enemy closer to the city, but allowed Jackson to strengthen his defenses. Each side would field a force of about 4,000 men. Jackson carefully used the geography of the area to best advantage, especially the swamps and Mississippi River. The British were obliged to charge the American lines in a frontal assault. The final encounters which began on the foggy morning of January 8, 1815, saved the nation's pride and spawned a legend. The combination of grapeshot and musket balls at close range proved devastating, the ground soon covered in red coats and blood. The British sustained over 2,000 casualties, including their commanding officer, General Edward Packenham, while the Americans lost fewer than one hundred men. Jackson had assembled a marginally trained army of farmers, city dwellers, criminals, and Indians—a multi-racial legion that represented the American republic in 1815. Those soldiers, with little chance of victory against seasoned Napoleonic veterans, struck one of the few resounding blows for the nation in the War of 1812. The peace treaty ending the conflict had been signed at Ghent, Belgium on Christmas Eve of 1814, some two weeks before the battle occurred. That meant little to victory-starved Americans, who wildly cheered their democratic army and its courageous frontier commander.[10]

Almost immediately after the battle, as the Hero of New Orleans basked in the glory of his triumph, composers seized the moment and taverns echoed with songs praising Old Hickory. "Jackson is the Boy" was among the most celebrated:

> Come all ye sons of freedom, Come all ye brave who lead 'em
> Come all who say God speed 'em, And sing a song of joy!
> To Jackson ever brave, Who nobly did behave—
> Unto Immortal Jackson, the British turned their backs on,
> He's ready still for action, O Jackson is the boy. . . .

Several years after the war, public enthusiasm for Jackson still had not waned, so Samuel Woodworth, a New England poet, penned "The Hunters of Kentucky," a song honoring the heroes of New Orleans. The melodious tune became immensely popular and a campaign standard during Jackson's run for the presidency in 1828. While emphasizing the role of the sharpshooters of the state, the lyrics made repeated reference to the General's leadership with stanzas such as:

> I suppose you've read in all the prints how Packenham attempted
> To make Old Hickory Jackson wince, but soon his schemes repented
> For we with rifles ready cocked, thought such occasion lucky,
> And soon around the general flocked the hunters of Kentucky.

More than a century later, Arkansas teacher Jimmy Driftwood wrote a piece in tribute to the success of American arms, entitled "The Battle of New Orleans." Recorded by country artist Johnny Horton, the track improbably reached number one on the national popular music charts in 1959. The song began with the lines:

> In 1814 we took a little trip
> Along with Colonel Jackson down the mighty Mississip
> We took a little bacon and we took a little beans
> And we fought the bloody British in a town in New Orleans.[11]

Old Hickory and his supporters, eager to promote a positive image amidst controversy, also crafted what evolved into one of the first campaign biographies. Such publications would later become commonplace in American politics. Major John Reid, Jackson's aide-de-camp during the War of 1812, and Tennessee comrade John Henry Eaton penned a four hundred-page tribute to their hero's military genius. Entitled *The Life of Andrew Jackson,* the reader learned almost exclusively about the general's exploits against the Creeks and the British. Jackson wanted to insure his legacy through a quality product that would gain wide distribution along the East coast, so he contacted accomplished Philadelphia author and publisher Mathew Carey in the summer of 1815. Two years later, Carey printed the first edition. As Jackson's political star ascended, however, Eaton made significant revisions to the text that removed any possible flaws from Jackson's character or decision-making, fashioning an even more appealing public figure for the presidential campaigns of 1824 and 1828.[12]

While Jackson's feats at New Orleans have been trumpeted over time in a variety of songs, poems and plays, there was a darker side to the Louisiana saga. When the general arrived in December, he found a city in a state of near panic. Jackson soon determined that he needed to deal with an unsettled and fearful business community, potentially disloyal elements among the citizenry, a disorganized military, and an uncooperative legislature. The chaotic situation demanded an approach similar to that exercised with his own troops in the recent Creek War. On December 16, he brought down a heavy hand and declared martial law. While such action might be justified for the next month, or at least until the British evacuation of Louisiana could be confirmed, Jackson extended military rule until March 13, 1815. Only word that the Ghent accord had been approved by Congress compelled the general to relinquish arbitrary power. While appreciating his contributions, New Orleans residents soon wearied of Jackson's censorship, arrests, trials, and banishments. His biographer Remini agreed that Jackson's behavior was "highhanded, bizarre, and dangerous." The Madison administration heard the protests regarding Jackson's conduct, but were hesitant to publicly chastise a national hero.

Of course, the general made no apologies for his actions, arguing that law and order must be maintained until formal notification arrived that the war had ended and the city no longer threatened. He remained in New Orleans until early April, enjoying the company of Rachel and five-year-old Andrew. In spite of the friction with the locals, the Jacksons were feted and honored at numerous festivities.

Understanding the relationship between Andrew and Rachel in this micro-environment, and their wider bond, is critical to comprehending Jackson and his behavior. From its public face, Jackson's passion and fierce loyalty to his wife prompted his involvement in a series of duels and brawls that were life-threatening, damaged his reputation, and became perpetual fodder for his political enemies. Privately, the couple's intense commitment, mirrored in their letters, reveals a perpetually lonely Rachel whose repeated pleas for her husband to abandon his military wanderings and return to the Hermitage were met with patriotic rationalizations. Jackson recognized her needs, and reassured her of his parallel desire to be nothing more than a Tennessee planter. In reality, he struggled rather unsuccessfully to balance his ambition and obsession with the nation's defense with his dedication to family.

Rachel no doubt prayed that the conclusion of the war with Britain would allow the Jacksons the opportunity for a respite from the stress and strain of separation, and she could finally take some pleasure in their mutual sacrifice. Now 47, she arrived in stylish New Orleans more the western farm wife than the southern plantation mistress. Unfashionably tanned and somewhat chubby—one observer referred to her as "a short, fat dumpling"—her dress was cotton not silk. Rachel squeezed into gowns, danced, dined, and experienced life in a large city for the first time. Shocked by the wickedness and splendor of New Orleans, she seemed both amused and overwhelmed.

The celebrations continued when the Jacksons arrived back in Nashville on May 15, but Andrew soon headed east to combat the negative rumors regarding his authoritarian rule. He journeyed to Washington in November, and received confirmation from Secretary of War Alexander J. Dallas that his reputation was still intact. The general's public image suffered no immediate damage from the decisions made to administer New Orleans in time of crisis. However, for those in Washington who supervised and observed his conduct, as well as the soldiers who served with and under him, a clear pattern of behavior had emerged. The Constitution, civil law, and individual rights mattered to Jackson, but not as much as the safety and security of the Union and the American people. The War of 1812 would not be the last time the general liberally interpreted the Constitution, or issued questionable orders to secure what he believed to be the greater good. His enemies, then and later in his career, viewed his acts as illegal, tyrannical, and despotic. While their arguments often rang true, condemning a patriotic warrior who repeatedly and successfully answered his country's call proved a difficult task indeed. The war had catapulted Jackson from a controversial frontier general to a national figure—"the Hero of New Orleans." Many enthusiastically made the comparison to George Washington and talked about rewarding Jackson with the White House.[13]

The administration in Washington had other priorities. Madison needed a man of his proven courage and standing to lead the army after the War of 1812. Accordingly, Jackson received the appointment as commander of the Southern Division, the region still rife with problems involving the Spanish and Indians. The choice came with foreseeable issues. Old Hickory, proud and prickly, soon involved himself in squabbles with the War Department over issues of power and control. These were not Jackson's finest moments. When James Monroe, whom Jackson had endorsed almost a decade earlier for the presidency, triumphed in 1816, the general hoped the tensions with Washington might ease.

And so they did. With the Virginian Monroe in the White House and South Carolinian John C. Calhoun leading the War Department, a more cooperative environment was established, and mutual goals could be advanced. Calhoun would develop the policy that provided the foundation for a practical process of Indian removal across the Mississippi River to new homes primarily in Oklahoma. In the meantime, Jackson busied himself with the oversight of treaty negotiations that ceded millions of acres of Cherokee, Chickasaw, and Choctaw lands in the Southwest. Those farmers who cheered the general's battlefield victories boisterously shouted his name when they learned of the new opportunities now afforded them to build their future on the frontier.

For many planters, diplomats, and generals, no objective loomed larger on that frontier than Florida. It was an outlaw's paradise. Jackson's Pensacola incursion of 1814 did not lead to an assertion of Spanish authority, rather it revealed Madrid's weakness in controlling the peninsula. Jackson firmly believed that hostilities in the region would not end until Spain ceded the territory to the United States. The problems were threefold. The Seminoles, a small (7,000) but hostile tribe, raided across the border into Georgia, burning farms, and stealing slaves and animals. Just as troubling, the territory was infested with smugglers and pirates, especially the area around Amelia Island on the Atlantic coast. Finally, Florida had become a haven for escaped slaves and displaced Creeks seeking asylum from their American pursuers. An abandoned earth and timber citadel on the Apalachicola River, called the Negro Fort, offered the fugitives sanctuary. The sizeable structure, some sixty miles from the U.S. border, was defended by a dozen cannons, and housed upwards of three hundred men well-armed with British muskets and powder.[14]

Florida's issues could be addressed by the American military, but they had no legal authority to cross the border. The peaceful purchase or cession of the peninsula seemed far in the distance, so Jackson would have welcomed a war enabling the U.S. to gain not only Florida, but Cuba as well. Jackson's appointment as commander of the Southern Division enabled him to stay informed about the inflamed Florida frontier. The general argued, and Washington agreed, that action must be taken. Accordingly, in the summer of 1816, he dispatched General Edmund P. Gaines to deal with the imminent problem of the Negro Fort. Old Hickory adjudged that the fortification "had been established by some villains for the purpose of murder, rapine, and plunder" and must be destroyed. Most white southerners would have agreed. An extended campaign might have been difficult and costly, but fortunately for the Americans, a gunboat reached the stronghold in late July and fired a lucky hot shot that ignited the fort's powder store. The ensuing explosion killed 270 of the occupants, and in one bloody blow eliminated both a shelter and a threat.

On Amelia Island, off the Atlantic coast near St. Augustine, the freebooting atmosphere worsened in the summer of 1817, as filibustering pirates, criminals, and slave traders gained control, and claimed the territory as part of the Mexican Republic. In November, out of patience with the turmoil, a frustrated Monroe administration sent General Gaines to restore order on the island. His brief, successful campaign once again violated Spanish sovereignty, but resolved yet another American problem.[15]

By 1818, Spain's imperial crisis seemed only to deepen. Her Latin American colonies remained in revolt, and the Crown had neither men nor resources to deal effectively with peripheral issues in Florida. Secretary of State John Quincy Adams had entered the picture, pressing the Spanish to ease their burden by simply allowing the U.S. to purchase the colony. While Adams attempted a soft approach, Secretary Calhoun in the War Department conveyed the orders to Jackson "to concentrate your forces and to adopt the necessary measures to terminate a conflict" which President Monroe had hoped to avoid. That conflict focused upon the seemingly endless Seminole raids which inflamed the border. Jackson's orders permitted him to enter Florida "to chastise the ruthless savages who have been depredating on the property & lives of our citizens," but explicitly warned against engaging Spanish troops or property. What if the Indian miscreants took shelter in Pensacola or St. Augustine? The entire U.S. offensive would be undermined. Why not take a different, more subtle course of action, Old

Hickory inquired? If Monroe granted him an "unofficial approval," Jackson would seize and hold the entirety of East Florida "as an indemnity for the outrages of Spain upon the property of our citizens." He assured the White House that this could be accomplished in 60 days.[16]

Whether Monroe formally endorsed Jackson's ambitious plan is the subject of considerable historical controversy. Jackson claimed that the assurance arrived in a February 1818 letter written by Tennessee Congressman John Rhea. The president denied he had told Rhea that Jackson could exercise broad powers to take control of the territory. Regardless, neither Monroe nor Calhoun restricted Jackson's moves. Both well knew, in a vacuum of specific instructions, the general would act aggressively. Jackson had made clear his personal feelings and intentions, and believed that Washington backed his position. The administration wanted to ensure that should the unpredictable Old Hickory embarrass the government, and he most certainly did so, the executive would be in a position to disavow any direct responsibility.

Jackson's force of about 2,000 U.S. army regulars, Tennessee militia, and friendly Creeks crossed into west Florida in March 1818. The First Seminole War had begun. The three-month expedition resulted in the Americans burning Indian villages, executing hostile chiefs, and temporarily seizing the Spanish town of St. Marks. The Seminoles occasionally skirmished with the Creeks, but generally remained elusive, one step ahead of the eastward-moving American column. Jackson's stated goal was the capture of one of the more powerful chiefs, Bowlegs, and the destruction of his town. After a 100-mile trek from St. Marks, in April Jackson's men did take and burn the village. A brief engagement with the Indians produced a few casualties, but Bowlegs and his followers escaped. Old Hickory and his soldiers had little interest in pursuing the Indians into the scrub pine and palmetto thickets of south Florida. Better to declare victory and go home.

Thus far, Jackson had only incurred the wrath of the Spanish government by his invasion and occupation of St. Marks. The international temperature would be ratcheted up dramatically, however, by his actions before he departed the territory. Jackson believed that the British played a major role in advising, arming, and supplying the Indians all along the frontier. Florida was no exception. Rumors regarding His Majesty's officers and agents abounded, and Jackson's suspicions were confirmed when two intriguers were captured. Alexander Arbuthnot, a seventy-year-old Scots trader, had been taken in St. Marks, and Robert Ambrister, a young army officer, apprehended at Bowlegs town. Jackson determined that they should be given a military trial for inciting and aiding the Seminoles. Arguably, both men were culpable, but whether they, as foreign nationals, could be charged in an American court on Spanish territory was improbable—and illegal. In somewhat typical fashion, Jackson ignored the legal protocol, determined that both were "unprincipled villains," and a military court found them guilty. Arbuthnot was hanged and Ambrister shot.

As a parting gesture, Jackson also seized Pensacola, encountering little resistance, in late May. He fully intended to leave behind a garrison in the town, as well as in St. Marks and at the site of the old Negro Fort. He considered each a trouble spot and all were within Spanish territory. Pleased with the outcome of recent months, Jackson returned to Tennessee, while the ripple effects of his brief Florida campaign redounded from Washington to London and Madrid and back again. Perhaps Monroe had been right in not taking full responsibility for his general's conduct.[17]

Notes

1 Jackson, June 4, 1812, to Willie Blount, *Jackson Papers*, II, 300–01; Jackson, November 12, 1812, to Tennessee volunteers, ibid., 342–43; AJ, November 29, 1812, to George Washington Campbell, ibid., 343–45; John Armstrong, February 6, 1813, to AJ, ibid 361; James Wilkinson, March 16, 1813, to AJ, ibid., 389; AJ, March 22, 1813, to James Wilkinson, ibid., 396–97.
2 Jackson, March 4, 1813, to William B. Lewis, ibid., II, 377–78; Rachel Jackson, February 8, April 5, 1813, to Jackson, ibid., 361–62, 400; Andrew Jackson, March 15, March 21, 1813, to Rachel Jackson, ibid., 387; Jackson, April 24, 1813, to John Armstrong, ibid., 403–04.
3 T.H. Benton, June 15, 1813, to Jackson, ibid., 406–07; Marquis James, *The Life of Andrew Jackson* (New York: Bobbs–Merrill, 1938), 150–52; Robert Remini, *Andrew Jackson and the Course of American Democracy* (New York: Harper and Row, 1984), 180–86.
4 Remini, *American Empire*, 187–233; David and Jeanne Heidler, eds., *Indian Removal* (New York: Norton, 2007), 9–13; David and Jeanne Heidler, *Old Hickory's War: Andrew Jackson and the Quest for Empire* (Mechanicsburg, PA: Stackpole Books, 1996), 12–22; Jackson, December 6, 1813 to William Martin, *Jackson Papers*, II, 470–74; Jackson, December 14, 1813, to Rachel, ibid., 486–87.
5 Remini, *American Empire*, 193–94, 210; Mark R. Cheathem, *Andrew Jackson: Southerner* (Baton Rouge: Louisiana State University Press, 2013), 80; Jackson, November 4, December 19, December 29, 1813, to Rachel Jackson, *Jackson Papers*, II, 444, 494, 515–16; Jackson, January 28, February 1, February 21, 1814, to Rachel, ibid., III, 21, 23–24, 35; Jackson, March 26, June 2, 1818, to Rachel, ibid., IV, 185, 213; Jackson, January 4, 1814, to Robert Hay, ibid., III, 8.
6 Jackson, April 1, July 16, August 10, 1814, to Rachel, ibid., 54–55, 89, 114; Jackson, May 7, 1818, to William Rabun, ibid., 201–02.
7 Heidlers, *Old Hickory's War*, 22–27; David and Jeanne T. Heidlers *Indian Removal* (New York: Norton, 2007), 56–59; Jackson, August 5, August 23, 1814, to Rachel, *Jackson Papers*, III, 104–05, 117; Jackson August 24, 1814, to M.G. Manrique, ibid., 119–21; Jackson, August 25, 1814, to John Armstrong, ibid., 122–23; Jackson October 26, 1814, to James Monroe, ibid., 173–74.
8 Remini, *American Empire*, 234–45; James, *Andrew Jackson*, 179–99; Brand, *Andrew Jackson*, 236–46; Jackson, November 6, 1814, to M.G. Manrique, *Jackson Papers*, III, 179–80.
9 Remini, *American Empire*, 246–54.
10 Ibid., 255–97; Brands, *Andrew Jackson*, 263–84; James, *Andrew Jackson*, 240–49.
11 Remini, *American Empire*, 296.
12 Jackson, August 28, 1815, to Mathew Carey, *Jackson Papers*, III, 379–80; Frank W. Owsley, Jr., ed., John Reid and John Henry Eaton, *The Life of Andrew Jackson* (Philadelphia: M. Carey, 1817).
13 Matthew Warshauer, "Andrew Jackson and the Legacy of the Battle of New Orleans" in Sean Patrick Adams, *A Companion to the Era of Andrew Jackson* (Malden, MA: Blackwell, 2013),

79–87; Remini, *American Empire,* 308–20; Brands, *Andrew Jackson,* 284–99; James, *Andrew Jackson,* 250–84.
14 Edmund P. Gaines, May 14, 1816, to Jackson, *Jackson Papers,* IV, 30–31.
15 Jackson, September 6, 1816, to Thomas S. Jesup, ibid., 60; John Caldwell Calhoun, December 26, 1817, to Jackson, ibid., 163–64; Remini, *American Empire,* 344–45; Brands, *Andrew Jackson,* 307–08; Cheathem, *Southerner,* 69–72.
16 John C. Caldwell, December 26, 1817, to Jackson, *Jackson Papers,* IV, 163; Jackson, January 6, 1818, to James Monroe, ibid., 366–67.
17 James, *Andrew Jackson,* 285–86; Brands, *Andrew Jackson,* 322–31; Heidlers, *Indian Removal,* 17–19; Heidlers, *Old Hickory's War,* 136–76; Jackson, May 5, 1818, to J.C. Calhoun, *Jackson Papers,* IV, 197–200; Jackson, June 2, 1818, to James Monroe, ibid., IV, 213–15.

CHAPTER **3**

THE ROAD TO THE PRESIDENCY (1819–1828)

In late June 1818, Jackson returned to Nashville with a host of admirers and almost as many enemies. He caused quite a stir, first in New Orleans, then in Florida. The heated political climate alerted White House aspirants that they needed to be wary of a new rival. Destroying Jackson's career and reputation would help any number of contenders in Congress and the administration. In London and Madrid, politicians and diplomats demanded answers, apologies, and indemnities for the reckless behavior of the general. Since the Monroe administration was unprepared and unwilling to take the blame for Jackson's actions, Spanish Minister Don Luis de Onís demanded to know what punishment would be meted out to the errant warrior. As Secretary of State Adams wisely observed, "The storm is rapidly thickening."

Monroe met with his advisors for a week in mid-July to sort out the responsibility. Eager to avoid any conflict with either Spain or Great Britain, the president and his cabinet found comfort in faulting Jackson. Secretary of the Treasury Crawford and Secretary of War Calhoun, both with an eye towards the presidency, urged a repudiation of Old Hickory and the evacuation of the Spanish forts. Monroe agreed. He attempted to distance himself from Jackson, rightfully fearing that his commander would be reprimanded for what amounted to acts of war upon a friendly power.

Perhaps no cabinet member had more at stake in this crisis than John Quincy Adams. He had been hesitant to recognize the independence of rebellious Spanish colonies in Latin American nations, worried that the Crown would retaliate by blocking the secretary's efforts to acquire Florida. In this tense atmosphere, he emerged as the only cabinet member to challenge the president and his colleagues. Adams believed correctly that Jackson's exploits had embarrassed Madrid and proved conclusively Spain's inability to control Florida's border. He argued that the general had violated no formal instructions and that necessity justified his course. Jackson should not be censured, although the properties seized should be returned. This compromise failed to satisfy the incensed Spanish, who insisted the officer be disciplined and his actions disavowed. Adams's trepidation over the fate of negotiations for the cession of the peninsula now seemed very real.

Instead of retreating in the face of the threats, Adams charged ahead. The U.S. would make no apologies for Jackson's conduct; instead, the secretary praised Old Hickory for acting in the defense of his country. He reiterated that Spanish administrators were incapable of crushing any nefarious activity in Florida which spilled over into the southern states. They, not Jackson, should be punished for incompetence or duplicity. And if the chaos and violence continued, Adams warned, the Spanish could expect Washington to take similar measures.

The secretary's bold position prevailed. Great Britain certainly did not want a war over the deaths of two subjects who held no official position in Florida, and Spain could not back up her strident posture without London's support. Talks over the transfer resumed, and on February 22, 1819, Adams and Onís signed the Transcontinental Treaty. The agreement ceded the Floridas to the U.S.: "East Florida," from St. Augustine to the Perdido River, and "West Florida," from the Perdido to the Mississippi River. The Sabine River marked the boundary between Louisiana and Spanish-held Texas, then the treaty line extended northwest to the Pacific Ocean. The Spanish wanted to guard against a probable American push into the Southwest from the Louisiana Purchase. Madrid received no direct monetary compensation, but the U.S. did agree to pay $5 million in claims that American citizens had against Spain for violations of neutral shipping rights on the high seas in the Napoleonic Wars. The treaty satisfied a long-term American quest for security, if not tranquility, on its southern border. The Spanish were gone, but the troublesome Seminoles remained.[1]

Old Hickory was a physical wreck. He had returned from the Seminole War weak and emaciated, coughing up blood, and with severe pain in his left side. The wearying ordeal and accompanying poor diet exacted their toll. Yet he took comfort in the success of his Florida operation. The conflict had virtually eliminated any immediate threat from Indians or their European allies. He was convinced that peace would exist along the southern frontier as long as the government occupied the forts he had seized. But could the administration or the Spanish be trusted? Jackson had his doubts.

Monroe attempted to handle his excitable general with sensitivity. The president reassured Jackson that he had confidence in the logic and legality of his movement across the border in pursuit of the Seminoles. On the other hand, in attacking and inhabiting Spanish property, Jackson had "transcended the limit" of his orders. Monroe could not defend holding their towns and forts. The possessions would be returned to Spain as a sign of good faith and inducement for a negotiated transfer of Florida to the U.S. Monroe warned Jackson that charges might be leveled against him for the abuse of his authority, and not just from the Spanish. While the administration and Jackson tried to reconcile their differences, particular congressmen picked up the torch, intending to burn the intractable general for his misdeeds. They demanded accountability for perceived violations of the war-making powers of the Constitution.

This simply would not do. Jackson fired back a lengthy defense of his role in the affair, arguing that his orders had been "comprehensive" and that he had "the fullest discretion" to carry out the campaign as he determined. Even so, if objections were raised from any quarter, he would gladly accept the responsibility. "I have never shrunk from it," he defiantly told Monroe, "and never will."[2]

The Florida controversy would not die. In November 1818, the president's annual message to Congress attempted to quiet the matter and assure the nation that Old Hickory had behaved in a patriotic manner. Some members of the cabinet and Congress remained unconvinced. When both Houses decided to investigate the incursion in January 1819, Jackson hurried to Washington to defend his reputation. He cautioned Monroe that a coalition, led by Secretary Crawford and Speaker of the House Henry Clay, was organizing to undermine his bid for a second term in 1820 as well as to discredit the general. The Tennessean was well aware of Crawford's "implacable hostility" and deemed Clay "a base unprincipled man." Both were ambitious, and Jackson likely stood in their way.

The Committee on Military Affairs of the House of Representatives, largely aligned with Jackson's enemies, reported on January 12 that the general had indeed exceeded his orders, especially by executing the two British subjects, Arbuthnot and Ambrister. The ensuing broader debate in the House included Clay's lengthy speech on January 20. The speaker attacked Jackson's conduct in Florida, his callous dealings with the Creeks, and hinted that the general was a power-hungry military chieftain.

For two weeks Jackson directed the forces of rebuttal from his Washington hotel room. On February 8, the votes on each of the four measures critical of Jackson failed by almost two to one. A Senate Committee, led by Crawfordite Abner Lacock of Pennsylvania, also reported a measure condemning the officer for occupying the Spanish posts, executing British subjects, and speculating in Florida lands. The administration forces stalled the bill until March 4 when Congress adjourned.[3]

Jackson emerged from the Washington wars bruised but triumphant. The Senate ratified the Adams-Onís Treaty in February, and Jackson's contribution to the settlement was duly noted by celebrations in his honor in Baltimore, Philadelphia, and New York. Congress had failed to brand him with any charges. Meanwhile, Speaker Clay scrambled to reassure Jackson that his speech attacking him on the floor of the House was not based on politics or personal advantage. Old Hickory was having none of it. He remained confident that Crawford drafted the literary fodder for "the vindictive, false, and malevolent" attacks on him, while "the insidious Mr. Clay" provided the public voice. Both men would remain his enemies, and there was no path to redemption. As Jackson assured a confidante, "Like Lucifer they have politically fallen never to rise again."

He was sorely mistaken. In little more than a decade, Crawford died, but Clay went on to a distinguished career as secretary of state and senator, twice challenging Jackson for the White House. As for the president, Monroe tentatively decided it best to reestablish his bond with Jackson. The chief executive's summer tour of the South and West had not originally included Nashville, but second thoughts prevailed. In early June, Monroe visited Jackson and inspected the "Hermitage," then under construction. The two took an improbable tour of the Shaker community near Lexington, Kentucky. Not surprisingly, Jackson had little use for the utopians or their religious attitudes.

Old Hickory battled more demons than the Shakers' unorthodox view of God. Though in fragile health, he felt compelled to spend too much time preparing written defenses of his actions in Florida. These tracts would be safeguards against future personal attacks. Moreover, by September 1819, the "treacherous" Spanish stalled their ratification of the treaty, prompting Jackson to doubt whether they would ever do so. The implosion of the process would inevitably result in a war between the U.S. and Spain, Jackson grumbled. The administration would regret abandoning the posts that he had dutifully seized in 1818, and would have to take again.

Despite his poor constitution, Jackson decided to remain in the army and prepare for a new campaign. He informed Monroe in November, "I cannot bare [sic] the idea of abandoning you, so long as you may think my services may be necessary for my country—and this I never will do without your consent." He asserted that if war did occur, Florida could be taken in three months and Cuba in just twice that time. Should Texas be grabbed as well? Jackson pondered the prospect, but decided it was not included within the 1819 treaty boundary. Besides, Texas was a territory "we could well do without"—for the present. Fortunately for both Spain and the U.S., in October 1820, Madrid finally signed the pact, but Florida remained on Jackson's horizon.[4]

The accompanying Indian issue was never far from Jackson's mind, nor from that of Secretary of War Calhoun. After an inept performance in the

War of 1812, the War Department desperately needed a reformer. It found one in the South Carolinian. The question of how to deal with the Indians east of the Mississippi River posed a primary challenge. For many Americans, especially along the frontier, the natives presented a persistent problem because of the physical threat of violence, the possibility of allying with ambitious European powers, and their sitting on valuable grain and cotton land. Calhoun and Jackson also recognized that contact with whites was changing, if not destroying, Indian culture. As paternalists, who believed strongly in white superiority, they argued that the Indians should not be considered as independent nations, but governed in the natives' own best interest by a more knowledgeable Washington. Although inferior, they had the capacity to improve under the proper white guidance.

Since the two societies struggled to coexist, assimilation or removal presented the two viable options. Assimilation would amount to "cultural genocide," while removal would at least allow them to maintain their language and customs. Calhoun crafted a policy in 1818 that offered both northern and southern Indians voluntary removal to lands largely in Oklahoma and Kansas. The secretary of state indicated that the new territories would be sparsely populated, and be home to sufficient animal life to sustain the new settlers. Their journey would be financially aided by the government, which would also provide the tribes with education and training.

Calhoun's Indian plans, humane for the time, also included reforms of native-white trade relationships. The goals included eliminating the abuses of liquor and government corruption, and promoting fairness and protection for the Indian. The secretary's proposals resulted in forty-one negotiated cessions and the exchange of millions of acres during his tenure (1817–1825). Appointed as an envoy, Jackson (Sharp Knife) brokered a treaty in October 1818 with the Chickasaw who ceded lands in Kentucky and Tennessee. The Treaty of Doak's Stand, signed in October 1820 with the Choctaw, resulted in the exchange of five million acres in Mississippi for 13 million acres across the river. Delighted residents named the state capital after the general.[5]

After almost a decade of government service as soldier, Indian fighter, and diplomat, it appeared in 1821 that Jackson might actually seek retirement in Tennessee. The owner of forty-four slaves and a thousand acres, the wealthy planter had nearly completed his Federal-style brick showplace, the Hermitage. The Jacksons, both 54 years old, remained geographically very close to where they had started their relationship more than three decades ago. Yet they had changed dramatically. Rachel found tranquility in her faith. Now a devout Presbyterian, she encouraged her adopted nephew, Andrew Jackson Donelson, to follow in her path. "Pure and undefiled religion is the greatest treasure on earth," Rachel assured him. Old Hickory had other instructions for the lad, encouraging his study of the law, and honing his skills in writing and debate. "Nothing tends more to expand the mind, and improve the intellect," he counseled, "than writing and investigating various subjects, it gives to thought a wide range."

Seemingly recollecting his own remarkable childhood, Jackson shared moral advice as well. Beware of dissipation, vice, and folly, he cautioned Andrew. "Innocent amusement" and social mixing with the "better class of society," individuals of "virtue and upright conduct," was time well spent. Jackson, whose letters rarely reflected the sense of humor of his youth, commented with some irony on the need to associate only with virtuous females, who would "enoble [sic] the mind, cultivate your manners," and prepare him "for the achievement of everything great, virtuous and honorable." Donelson should avoid the less chaste as a "viper" who would engender corruption, and contaminate his morals. Such counsel came from the man who once invited prostitutes to a Christmas party.[6]

Jackson's principles were tested at other levels as well. More than once on the battlefield, his unfailing patriotism and dedication to the Union had been demonstrated. He thought the nation indivisible, but provided a strong role for the states. For example, he believed it unconstitutional for Washington to engage in the construction of internal improvements such as roads or canals. These projects should be left to the states. Indeed, Jackson applauded Monroe's veto in May 1822 of a measure to use federal dollars to fund the Cumberland Road between Maryland and Illinois.

To his consternation, the nation began splintering over the issue of slavery in the expanding West. The Compromise of 1819–1821 ultimately allowed for the admission of Missouri as a slave state, Maine as a free state, and the division of the Louisiana Purchase into free and slave territory at the line 36° 30' latitude, the southern boundary of Missouri. As the debate and the proposed Missouri state constitution moved through Congress, northerners rejected the prohibitions Missourians placed on the entrance of free blacks into the state. As a defender of slavery and states' rights, an angry Jackson chided the Yankees for their meddling. "The Northern people have fully unmasked themselves," he observed. Fortunately, by late summer, the House of Representatives did resolve the slavery issue, at least temporarily. Even so, Jackson was suspicious of the power of Congress to do mischief. Rather than agree that it represented the people, he contended that it must be held in check by the judicial and executive branches. Too much legislative power could well result in demagoguery and despotism.[7]

Meanwhile, Jackson continued to express concern about his somewhat battered reputation and how best to combat the presidential aspirations of "wicked" and corrupt William H. Crawford. In January 1821, the opportunity for personal vindication presented itself when Monroe offered Jackson the governorship of Florida. The president had first broached the subject in 1819, but the general expressed little interest. Now Jackson reconsidered. The congressional attempts to discredit him had failed, yet had still been made public. Perhaps exoneration and justice might best be assisted by demonstrating that the administration had confidence in his leadership. What more appropriate place would reflect that faith than Florida? Jackson resigned his commission in the army, accepting the governorship, and its $5,000 yearly salary, with a tone of self-sacrifice. He agreed to serve until January 1822 at the latest. His friends had persuaded him that he might hasten the organization of the new government. The end result would accelerate the growth of American settlers in the region. Only weeks after reaching the decision, however, he expressed second thoughts. Rachel had genuine reservations about the Florida climate, while Andrew himself had grown weary of public life. Even so, he could not retreat from his decision. Jackson had promised the president. He would accept the symbolic transfer of Florida from the Spanish, create a new democracy, and depart amidst applause from every quarter. What could possibly go wrong?[8]

The Jacksons, including Rachel and son Andrew, Jr., departed the Hermitage by steamboat on April 14, bound for New Orleans and then the Gulf coast of Alabama. By the end of the month, the new governor had arrived near Mobile. He commenced the exchange of letters with his predecessor, Colonel José Maria Callava, in Pensacola, that provided for the Spanish withdrawal from West Florida. A trusted Jackson lieutenant, Robert Butler, handled the cession of East Florida, administered separately in St. Augustine. The correspondence between Jackson and Callava did not go well. The general never trusted the Spanish. Callava fit the pattern of a Castilian officer who, Jackson believed, would lie or break promises. Both men had a strong sense of protocol and stronger egos. Jackson spoke no Spanish, and Callava no English.

In an effort to facilitate the transfer, Jackson dispatched two agents fluent in Spanish, Dr. James C. Bronaugh and Judge Henry Brackenridge, to deal with Callava. Their report was disheartening. The Americans prepared to whisk the governor and the two hundred Spanish troops quartered in the city off to Havana by U.S. transport, but Callava refused to leave until he received official orders from his superior in Cuba. That authorization would not arrive until June 9.

Uncomfortable in her surroundings, Rachel soon settled into housing in Pensacola, while formality and the icy relations between Jackson and Callava obliged Andrew to remain in camp about fifteen miles outside the city. Finally, on July 17, the transfer was enacted, the stars and stripes hoisted, and the Spanish departed. Perhaps now the Jacksons could celebrate the fruits of over two months of tedious delay and negotiation.[9]

Andrew and Rachel found themselves in an alien world. The natural beauty of their new environs delighted them. Rachel talked excitedly about the lushness of the flowers and abundance of fruits—oranges, peaches, grapes, and pomegranates. The water view and "exhilarating" sea breeze, she enthused, "enlivened the whole system."

However, there was much work to be done. Most of the houses in the city appeared in a state of neglect, dilapidated or in ruin, and the public squares overgrown with plant life. The oppressive heat and incessant rain, water running as much as two feet deep along the streets, made life uncomfortable and difficult. While the population increased with the arrival of each ship, for the present, most residents were dark-skinned, Catholic, and knew only Spanish and French.

Predictably, the reality of the transfer was met with anguish and tears. The new governor labored to set in motion a civilian government based on democratic principles. Undertaking the integration of American culture and laws into a Latin world, without the benefit of a printing press or extensive staff, was daunting. Jackson even began to study Spanish to help facilitate communication. Leadership in two critical areas was ensured by the appointments of Dr. Bronough to head the Board of Health and Judge Brackenridge as Pensacola's mayor.

Jackson predicted that, in time, Florida would become "a very important place" because of climate and geography. That future, however, would not deter his departure. Within weeks of taking office, he began to plan an autumn return to Nashville. From the moment of his acceptance of the post, Jackson had informed Monroe that his tenure would be brief. That view was likely confirmed by health problems, cultural shock, and particularly the lack of power to control the territory. Jackson wrongly assumed that the president would give him wide authority to shape policy. Instead, Monroe complicated the circumstances by not consulting the governor on numerous appointments, and making what Jackson considered to be weak choices. Perhaps Monroe had learned from the Seminole War that his general must be kept on a short political leash.[10]

Controversy often followed Jackson and his abbreviated stint as governor proved no exception. Before traveling to Tennessee in early October, he managed to spark an imbroglio that followed him into the upcoming presidential election. The somewhat convoluted situation involved certain legal documents in the possession of former Governor Callava, who had remained in Pensacola in a diplomatic capacity for the Madrid government. Callava refused to surrender the papers, so Jackson ordered the documents seized and the Spaniard thrown in jail. Jackson then defied a judge's writ of habeas corpus for Callava's release and new charges of Old Hickory's abuse of authority and power emerged. When the former governor was set free, he promptly proceeded to Washington to complain about his treatment.

The controversy swirled in congressional and diplomatic circles as well as in the press, placing the administration once again in the position of defending the conduct of its very aggressive officer. Monroe remarked on Jackson's "zeal and warmth" in pursuing "Spanish powers, too much in the Spanish way." Attorney General William Wirt mirrored the president's view of heavy-handed, arbitrary power, more explicitly seeing Jackson as violent and ignorant. Secretary Adams defended Jackson, as he had during the Seminole War. Eventually, the administration approved the general's conduct, but Congress's investigation considering his impeachment continued into March 1822 before the charges were dropped.

With no obvious successor to Monroe in sight, presidential fever had already begun to rise in the capital. A caucus of the members of the House and Senate, not popular conventions in the states, chose the candidates. Would Jackson have any cachet with Congress? His diplomatic experience was limited to Indian treaties and his political role to short-terms in both houses decades before. In contrast, his lack of formal education combined with his military adventures to create a bona fide frontier hero. For those eyeing a run for the White House in 1824, painting Jackson as less than iconic was just good politics. Too often, the impulsive general provided them with the brush.[11]

Jackson formally resigned the governorship in November 1821, but the chatter about a presidential run had emerged months before. Was he healthy enough for the office? He constantly complained about various maladies, from an ever-present cough, prompting the throwing up of "great quantities of fleme [sic]," to pain in his shoulder and back, and loose bowel problems (20 discharges in 12 hours). He seemed reconciled to the reality that his full strength would never return.

A letter from a Tennessee friend arrived in August, advising Jackson that his supporters in Pennsylvania had explored the political landscape and determined to advance his candidacy. Nashville newspapers gossiped about the possibility. A caucus of the state legislature made the matter official by endorsing him in the summer of 1822. Indian war companion Sam Houston assured Jackson that his rivals in Washington "will be frost bitten by the mere mention of your name." "You have friends throughout America," Houston raved. The next president would be "the People's choice."[12]

The people mattered to Jackson. He pondered how well would they be represented in a petty and small-minded Congress that had repeatedly attempted to attack and destroy his reputation. Party representatives would soon assemble in a Democratic-Republican caucus to determine the next president of the United States. The Federalists had failed to run a candidate in the 1820 contest, allowing Monroe to secure a second term unopposed. The winner of the caucus in 1824 would now likely become the next occupant of the White House. For Old Hickory, such a system denied fundamental principles of democracy and sound republican government. Where was the voice of the masses? Their will would certainly be thwarted if someone as corrupt as Crawford secured the nomination.

Accordingly, in 1822, Jackson began carefully monitoring the prospective candidates. As Crawford's political stock rose, Jackson became more serious about making his own entry into the race. His decision would not be based on advancing an agenda or rewarding supporters with patronage positions, he argued, but rather on restoring the integrity of the federal government that had been compromised under Monroe. The president was not evil, but he lacked firmness. His poor appointments and negligence had sunk his administration into a free-for-all plagued by favoritism and corruption.

While troubled by the plight of the government, Jackson's principles also held that exhibiting overt ambition and crafting deals was inappropriate behavior for someone seeking the nation's highest office. Consequently, he remained coy about a possible run, although his letters on the subject somehow found themselves into various newspapers. Jackson determined to exert no effort and remain "perfectly silent" on the matter. "I never have been a candidate for office, I never will," he explained to Richard Call. Yet, Jackson affirmed, the people of a republic have the right to appeal for a man's service, and he has an obligation to answer that appeal. Old Hickory would be the available man. He conceded that the nation did have viable alternatives. The populace would be well governed by either John Quincy Adams, "a candid independent man," or John C. Calhoun, "a highminded and honourable man." Henry Clay and "archfiend" William Crawford, who had repeatedly maneuvered to ruin Jackson's reputation, remained, of course, unacceptable.[13]

By 1823, in the whirligig of American politics, Andrew Jackson had once again become a problem. His unapologetic nationalism and bold, sometimes rash, behavior in defense of the country embarrassed the government, while endearing him to the common folk. Undoubtedly, Monroe heard voices from numerous quarters urging him to eliminate a presidential contender who was rapidly becoming the first popular hero since George Washington.

Latin America provided the perfect solution. In January, Jackson learned of his appointment and prompt Senate confirmation as first U.S. Minister to Mexico. While assuring Monroe that he interpreted the selection in the friendliest terms, he nonetheless graciously declined. After Mexico had won its independence from Spain in 1819, the resultant chaotic state of affairs had propelled Agustín de Iturbide into seizing the crown as emperor. Jackson disliked the Spanish, another of his prejudices, and assured Monroe that he could not in good conscience represent the U.S. to a dictator who would "rivet the chains of despotism upon his country." Nothing positive could come from any association with Iturbide, as it might be perceived as an endorsement of his rule. "I hate bowing to a Tyrant," Jackson proclaimed to his friend John Coffee. Had Mexico been ruled by republican forces and the people enjoyed free political will, he ventured, his decision may well have been different. Perhaps. It is difficult to imagine the Jacksons enjoying Mexico City under any circumstances, especially when the rising tide of popular sentiment was lifting his presidential possibilities.[14]

Jackson preferred to remain at the Hermitage, managing his property and worrying about any number of subjects, including his extended family, the political climate, and foreign affairs. He did not hesitate to offer his counsel to both family members and friends. Perhaps surprisingly for an unlettered frontiersman, he admonished his ward Anthony Wayne Butler, a student at Yale, that he could not approve limiting his course choices to the Classics. Mathematics was critical, Jackson contended, and "it is a thorough knowledge of the sciences that opens and expands the mind, and gives a proper erangement [sic] and system to argument." He concurrently lambasted Butler for his financial irresponsibility, resulting from spending beyond his annual $750 inheritance, a princely sum, and repeatedly asking Jackson for assistance. "It is easy to spend money," a piqued Jackson remarked, "but difficult to make it honestly."[15]

Old Hickory also dedicated time to politics, speaking specifically about his rivals, their strengths and weaknesses in various states and within the congressional caucus. He rightly saw that the candidacies of Clay and Crawford were doomed. Many Jeffersonians anticipated that Crawford would be the choice of the caucus, but the attachment to unsavory manipulation of the process by Washington insiders "would destroy the election of any man whose name is before the nation." Time and again, Jackson returned to the theme of the virtue and good sense of the people, and of his confidence in their judgment. Such views may appear naïve, or the cynic may argue that his claims of trust in the masses was for public consumption. Not so. Jackson repeatedly and consistently addressed the subject, convinced that "if uninfluenced by anything and left to their own reason, they will always decide right." With less confidence, he added, "I hope they will in the next presidential election."[16]

Jackson worried about the turmoil in Europe. He feared that the Holy Alliance of European monarchs—despots and tyrants—would unite to restore Spain's former colonies in South America. What would the United States do if the Europeans invaded? Their presence would threaten the hard-earned liberty of both the Latin Americans and the United States. The country must be prepared to defend itself. That defense included a concern about foreign bayonets on the Mexican border poised to strike at the American South and West as well as the need to protect Cuba from occupation. National security and prosperity demanded that the island not fall into the hands of any European power. "Our aid can prevent it, and we ought not to hesitate on this subject," he assured John C. Calhoun. As a result, he strongly sanctioned the president's message to Congress in December 1823, referred to later as the Monroe Doctrine, intended to discourage European meddling in western hemispheric affairs.[17]

The campaign did not proceed without a few potholes in the political road. In October 1823, the Crawford forces appeared poised to use the reelection of U.S. Senator John Williams, a Jackson critic, as a signal that Tennessee was divided over Old Hickory, and perhaps even backed the Treasury Secretary. Jackson's supporters attempted to engage other candidates as challengers to Williams. When that strategy failed, they placed their hero's name in nomination just a scant four days before the election.

Jackson narrowly won by a 35 to 25 vote, but was embarrassed by what appeared to be a sign of White House ambition. He felt obliged to rationalize the sequence of events, explaining to Calhoun, "Thus you see me a Senator contrary to my wishes, my feelings and my interests, to gratify the state in prostrating Crawfordism and the intrigues." For Jackson, the malice posed by a Crawford presidency trumped his hopes for remaining at the Hermitage, as the campaign played out with him in low profile. He no doubt did prefer Nashville, Rachel, and his crops, to Washington, alone, and exposed to the endless conniving and sordid deals. Jackson protested a return to public service, but as he told John Coffee, felt compelled to respond to the will of the people. Many would have argued that "that will" might have been manipulated by his supporters.[18]

Jackson headed to Washington in November 1823 with a heavy heart. He was reluctant to leave the Hermitage and Rachel, who was "more disconsolate than I ever knew her before." Jackson's absences had become commonplace and his tired rhetoric predictable. His marriage, his family, and his farm mattered, but the nation, and arguably his contribution to its future, mattered more. God had a plan—"purposes that his goodness has designed"—and Jackson believed that his life moved as part of that plan in a country with a destiny designed by Providence. He clearly missed Rachel's presence. "This separation has been more severe to me than any other," he complained, as he encouraged her to join him in Washington in the fall of 1824. That, too, was in God's hands, "If providence permits us again to unite we must travel together, and live together whilst permitted to remain Tennants here below."[19]

For the winter session, Jackson moved into a comfortable boarding house, operated by Mr. and Mrs. William O' Neale. Margaret, their young, attractive daughter, worked at the hotel, played piano, and entertained the family and guests. Her behavior soon scandalized the capital. Jackson occupied one half of the house with Tennessee Senator John Eaton and Congressman Richard Call. From that vantage point, the general watched and waited, evaluating the evolving presidential contest, and attending a grand ball given by John Quincy and Louisa Catherine Adams on January 8, the anniversary of the Battle of New Orleans. Jackson gathered information from various correspondents, carefully and continually analyzing the possibilities in each state. He quickly determined that the race had narrowed to Adams and himself.

Jackson also understood that he had an image problem. In a city filled with men of education and social pretension, he was the outsider, the barbarian. He held a tomahawk in one hand and knife in the other, an uncivilized soul of rash and vengeful temperament. While the savvy Jackson decried deal-making, he certainly dedicated a good deal of time to altering his persona. Appearing at few parties, he was not averse to private conversation aimed at healing the rifts between himself and numerous members of the capital's political establishment, including old adversary Thomas Hart Benton. Within a month, he believed inroads had been made, and confided to a friend, "I am getting on very smoothly."[20]

The Crawford forces remained undeterred by the general's best efforts. Crawford had suffered an apparent stroke in September 1823, leaving him physically and perhaps mentally impaired. Still, in February 1824, his backers proceeded with the congressional caucus. Jackson decried the gathering as an unconstitutional intrigue engineered by demagogues who denied the people the selection of their president. Corruption and bribery would follow as the masses lost faith in their government.

On the night of February 14, Jackson's long-standing prediction of the caucus's demise came true. Only 68 of a possible 261 Democratic-Republican congressmen and senators met to choose the party's nominee and 64 cast their votes for William H. Crawford. Congress had voted with its feet. Ignoring the outcome, numerous states held conventions to select candidates by popular acclaim. "This will be the last of King Caucus," Jackson exulted, "its Funeral Knell will be sounded throughout the union." Pennsylvania led the way on March 4, nominating Old Hickory for president.

Jackson obviously delighted in this democratic revolution and in his popularity. Yet he remained the reluctant candidate, averse to public life and willing to lead the nation only because the people called him to serve. His previous encounters with politics, especially in Washington, had embittered him. "I find mankind treacherous and corrupt," he lamented to his nephew, "and virtue to be found amonghst [sic] the farmers of the country alone." Jackson surveyed his campaign with great interest as it gathered momentum in state after state, largely at the expense of Calhoun and Crawford. Clay and Adams remained in the race, launching their own statewide efforts. Calhoun soon withdrew his candidacy, ultimately accepting the nomination to the rather unremarkable post of vice president.[21]

The Senate, with its attention focused upon the upcoming election, finally adjourned in late May, having accomplished little save a modest increase in the tariff. Jackson ruffled some feathers in the South when he favored the measure, arguing that it protected American agriculture and encouraged home markets. Although acting as the Chair of the Military Appropriations Committee, he delivered only four brief speeches in his six-month tenure. Most notably, on March 9, he supported a measure endorsing new guns for various forts. The relieved Tennessean departed the capital by the shortest route for Nashville, worn out by the endless debate over matters which he adjudged could be resolved in several hours. A man of few words and little patience, Jackson observed, "Nature never intended me for any such pursuit I am sure."

As the campaign progressed into the summer, potential issues such as tariffs, banking, and slavery took a backseat to personality and principles. Since Jackson spent minimal time in Congress and had not served abroad, his rivals attacked him for inexperience, as well as for his behavior and excesses in numerous adventures from New Orleans to Florida. The country could not be trusted to a military chieftain, they contended.

The American people listened—and widely rejected those arguments. They responded to Jackson not only as one of their own, a farm boy made good, but perhaps more importantly, responded to his unrivalled patriotism and courage in defense of his country. No one since George Washington had demonstrated such commitment over decades against the British and Indians. For his enemies to succeed, Jackson's character and reputation must be destroyed.[22]

Jackson's defense of his legacy became the cornerstone of his campaign. He was the one candidate, because of his limited political service, who was beyond partisanship and above corruption. He was the one to preserve the republican ideology of Jefferson, and restore liberty and virtue to the government and the people. Jackson became actively involved in the contest, writing numerous letters to supporters, rebutting attacks, planning strategy, and counting potential votes. Since the caucus rendered its judgment in February, and lacked modern technology, the candidates had little opportunity to put together a national organization. Instead, the election of

1824 was fought out at the state level where Old Hickory had broad-based backers who effectively utilized creative methods of campaigning. These included the extensive use of newspapers, a campaign biography lauding his military service, and even buttons with the image of the general to be worn on the lapel.[23]

The strategy worked. For the first time in U.S. history, voters selected the electors by popular ballot in twelve of the eighteen states. Andrew Jackson emerged the favorite. From Pennsylvania to Mississippi, the people rose to give Jackson more popular (153,000) and electoral (99) votes than his closest rival John Quincy Adams (114,000 and 84). Outside of New England, which held firm for Adams, Jackson proved to be truly a national candidate. He had taken eleven states. While his standing seemed undeniable, the division among the four contestants (including Clay and Crawford), denied Jackson an electoral majority. In February, the battle would go to the House of Representatives where each state would cast one vote for the presidency.

Old Hickory, accompanied by Rachel, travelled 28 days before reaching Washington and Gadsby's Hotel, William O'Neale's old property, on December 7, 1824. As he prepared to return to his Senate duties, Jackson took little opportunity to bask in the glow of his widespread support. Hundreds of callers and dozens of invitations inundated the Jacksons, but the general instructed his wife to maintain a low public profile—no balls, parties, or theaters. He likewise tried to avoid situations where the conversation would turn to the subject of the election. With apparently no resentment or regret, he fatalistically explained that if further intrigue denied him the White House, he would return to the Hermitage and his crops with comfort and relief.[24]

Under the Twelfth Amendment to the Constitution, when no candidate receives a majority of the electoral votes, the House of Representatives chooses the president from among the top three electoral candidates. The politicking during the month of January 1825 was frenetic and relentless, as each aspirant and his champions labored to shore up support or woo congressmen away from their original preference. Jackson, who opposed such "intrigues," felt compelled to take part in these activities, although his role was abbreviated by an untimely accident. After a late night conference at his hotel, Jackson stumbled on the top step of the stairs. His ensuing fall ripped open the old chest and shoulder wounds from his duels. Hemorrhaging badly and near death, he lay in bed for a week.

The outcome of the election on February 9 stunned both the candidates and the public. On the first ballot, Adams received the votes of thirteen states, Jackson garnered seven, and Crawford took four. The anti-Jacksonians had bargained effectively. Somehow the general lost the support of four states (Maryland, Illinois, North Carolina, and Louisiana) in the House where he had received their popular vote in November. Clay played a major role by engineering the transfer of the votes of Kentucky and Ohio (states that endorsed him) to Adams. Fair enough, one might argue, but in Clay's home state of Kentucky, Jackson was the clear preference if Clay withdrew.

The Jacksonians were well aware of the conversations, jockeying, and flurry of proposals for position and reward that had been made since the November balloting. They, too, had been courted by eager office-seekers. Speculation extended to the highest levels. Adams and Clay met on the evening of January 9, as John Quincy described, "in a long conversation explanatory of the past and prospective of the future." What did they discuss? Were promises made? There is no "smoking gun," and historians are sharply divided over whether the need for an explicit bargain even existed. The practical outcome was revealed, however, five days after the House balloting, when the new president named Clay as his secretary of state. Jackson needed no convincing. He had seen the reports in the press in late January that Clay had taken a public stand for Adams. That was unexpected and Jackson believed it would doom Clay, "He is greatly fallen, never to rise again in the estimation of the American nation."

Jackson had predicted the same outcome three years earlier. He never liked the Kentuckian, and Clay's self-promotion seemed in character. Adams, in contrast, had always been an able and honest man, but now had betrayed the public trust. The general lamented, "Intrigue, corruption, and the sale of public office is the rumor of the day." The manipulation of the states' votes was abhorrent and anti-democratic, but the reward for facilitating this denial of the people's will proved simply too much. Despite the rumors of a deal and the potential damage that would ensue to both their careers, Adams extended, and Clay accepted, the position that placed him in line to succeed to the White House. The present and future ambitions of both men trumped their political good sense. Reflecting upon the betrayal of Christ by one of his apostles, an infuriated Jackson told a close friend, "So you see the Judas of the West has closed the contract and will receive his thirty pieces of silver." The "corrupt bargain" had been sealed and the campaign of 1828 commenced.[25]

For Jackson, the principles of the republic had been betrayed. Only he could act to redeem the virtue of the revolutionary republic of the Founding Fathers. He arrived home in April, resigning his Senate seat in October 1825. Jackson wanted no confusion about exploiting his public office to promote a presidential bid—and that course had been decided upon. Fearing he might appear too ambitious and conniving, Jackson gave few public speeches outside Tennessee. One exception was the general's triumphant return to New Orleans for a January 8, 1828 celebration, offering the occasion for what has been described as the first presidential campaign speech.

Usually, however, he busied himself organizing a campaign team, the Nashville Central Committee or "Nashville Junto," consisting of such old Tennessee friends as John Eaton, John Overton, William B. Lewis, and Sam Houston. Newspapers were critical, so Jackson fired off letters to comrades that would find their way into editorials across the nation.

Health issues remained a concern. Jackson continued to suffer from the residue of carrying two lead bullets, one in the chest, the other below his shoulder, from the Dickinson and Benton encounters. He endured dysentery, rheumatism, bone deterioration, and pulmonary abscesses, frequently coughing up blood. The pain was palpable, the remedies often worse than the ailment. He drank the universal cure-all for the era, calomel, which contained mercury. He also consumed and bathed in sugar of lead (lead acetate), a common folk remedy. Over time, these toxic poisons took their toll and weakened his constitution. His health problems included the loss of many of his teeth, and a bad set of dentures made public speaking difficult. A series of maladies also plagued Rachel, especially lung and heart problems, thus keeping the Jacksons close to the Hermitage.

No matter. His views on various subjects of importance filtered out through the press. The extent to which a discussion of these issues trumped personality politics in 1828 remains the subject of serious debate. Jackson was at heart a man of conservative states' rights principles wrapped within a nationalist framework. John Quincy Adams offered the country a progressive and visionary agenda, including an observatory, national university, system of weights and measures, federally funded internal improvements, and global exploration. That vision stalled in Congress with Adams accomplishing little in his four White House years. While he represented the future, most Americans likely agreed with Jackson's notion that the primary goal of the government should be first to pay off the national debt and prepare for the country's defense before embarking on ambitious programs. If surplus revenue existed, he suggested that it be given to the states to educate the poor.

Jackson firmly believed the Indian must be removed to create a pathway for the growth of the country and prosperity for the American farmer. In negotiations for the Indians' land, they should be told the truth. He maintained in 1826 that lying and deception would serve no purpose. Rather, the Indians must realize that their lives and property would be exposed to white encroachment. This inevitability dictated the wisdom of removal to new lands across the Mississippi River. Indeed, the Indians should be shown their potential homes in order to ensure that they were satisfied with the treaty arrangements.

Jackson contended that internal improvements, the building of roads and canals, should be paid for by the state, if constructed within its borders.

Surplus federal government funds might be distributed to the states to build a road if it connected two states. Each state, however, must consent to the project and agree to fund the maintenance of its segment of the interstate road or canal.

The tariff also reemerged as a national controversy. What was fair in the North, which advocated higher rates and protection for American industry, might be unfair in the South, which sought lower rates to facilitate European commerce in agricultural products. Jackson, and Tennessee colleague John Eaton, were the only two southerners voting for the modest increases passed by Congress in 1824. When the rates were raised rather dramatically to an average of 45 percent in import duties in 1828, the so-called "Tariff of Abominations," Jackson equivocated. He told friends that calm and deliberate debate, mutual concessions made by North and South, and a "judicious" tariff should be the desired result. Perhaps, most importantly, Jackson trusted in the principle of a United States. "There is nothing that I shudder at more than the idea of a separation of the Union," he confessed to James Hamilton, Jr. For Old Hickory, the Union guaranteed liberty to the people; the state governments, in turn, protected the people against corruption and the mishandling of executive power.

In foreign affairs, Jackson endorsed the Monroe Doctrine and a defense of the hemisphere against European incursion. He had real objections, however, to a mission proposed by President Adams to send delegates to a Panama Congress in 1826 which might unite the nations of North and South America for purposes of security or trade. George Washington had cautioned against such an "entangling alliance" in 1796, and Jackson feared that war might result. He deemed such a gathering "a most dangerous and alarming scheme," rejoicing when the Senate delayed the mission for months. The delegates finally arrived in Central America after the congress adjourned.[26]

While Jackson's views on these major issues no doubt mattered to many Americans, the 1828 campaign was dominated by a return to the question of temperament and character. Old Hickory and his supporters repeatedly felt the need to defend his actions in New Orleans and during the Creek War. The Adams forces portrayed him as violent and out of control, seizing power and running roughshod over both civilians and soldiers. Charges were leveled that Jackson beat his slaves and had conspired with former vice president Aaron Burr in his plot to invade Mexican territory in 1805–1806. More troubling, in February 1827, the adulterous nature of his marriage exploded on the scene, as administration papers contended that Jackson had stolen Rachel from her husband. The Frankfort, Kentucky *Commentator* compared Rachel to "a dirty, black wench." A furious Jackson rushed to the defense of his wife and her reputation, penning letter after letter in response. Perhaps the low point came with the accusation that Jackson's mother Elizabeth was a prostitute brought to the U.S. by British soldiers. She had, they alleged, married a mulatto and had borne several children, Jackson being a product of that liaison.

The year 1828 witnessed an exponential rise in campaign organization and operation. President Adams attempted to position himself above the fray, but could not resist mocking Jackson's grammar, spelling, and use of the English language. The tactic backfired, as most Americans rejected Adam's intellectual posturing. The National Republicans wisely relied on the experience and boldness of Henry Clay and Massachusetts Senator Daniel Webster to lead the way in organizing their coalition and attacking Jackson.

Meanwhile, the Jacksonians had assembled their formidable combination, with the central committee headquartered in Nashville. As early as 1826, the campaign gained valuable allies, most importantly Senator Martin Van Buren. The New Yorker had been one of numerous Crawford supporters, including *Richmond Enquirer* editor Thomas Ritchie, who also came onboard. Ambition, blended with the realization that Jackson apparently shared many of their states' rights views, earned their endorsement. Vice President Calhoun perceived Jackson as philosophically compatible, prompting a guiltless shift in allegiance from Adams to Old Hickory. Calhoun placed himself in the unique position of becoming the vice presidential selection again in 1828, but this time as a Democrat.

A rivalry developed almost immediately between Calhoun and Van Buren to win the favor, indeed, inherit the mantle of the new "Jacksonian Democratic Party." The general's questionable health might throw either of them into the breach as early as 1832, and each determined that he would be ready. Their approval and activism gave Jackson strength in literally every state in the union outside of New England. In the short term, this alliance gained control of Congress in 1827, ensuring the defeat of any measure Adams might introduce.[27]

Popular politics reached new levels. Rallies, barbeques, and picnics become campaign essentials in small towns and cities across America. Patriotic citizens formed "Hickory Clubs" to extol the Tennessean's qualities. "The Hunters of Kentucky" could be heard emanating from tavern after tavern where bourbon-infused Jacksonians trumpeted their hero's victory at New Orleans. The whimsical song concluded not only with his triumph, but an admonition to the women of Louisiana to "Remember what our trade is, just send for us Kentucky boys, and we'll protect ye ladies."

A national network of newspapers, headed by such talented young editors as Amos Kendall and Francis P. Blair, reached the public in increasing numbers, along with various pamphlets and brochures. The Jacksonians returned repeatedly to the issues of the president's abuse of his office and the "corrupt bargain" between Adams and Clay. The level of civility was further lowered by accusing Adams of squandering $25,000 in government funds by purchasing games, especially an expensive billiard table, for the White House. A more outrageous assertion centered on John Quincy as a pimp. While Minister to Russia, he supposedly procured a young American woman for Czar Alexander I.[28]

As the election headed towards a triumphant outcome for the Democrats, tragedy struck. On June 1, Lyncoya died at the age of 16 in Nashville, apparently of a pulmonary condition. While some scholars argue that the boy had not received the degree of attention or affection Jackson dedicated to his other "sons," Andrew Jackson, Jr. and Andrew Jackson Hutchings, Lyncoya had been a vital part of the family since his infancy. He had received a solid education from private tutors and at Cumberland College. Jackson tried, but failed, to secure him a place at West Point. Instead, the youth became a saddler's apprentice and was learning the trade when he died. Rachel was devastated, while Jackson made no mention of his passing in his letters. His silence may speak volumes regarding his feelings.[29]

The 1828 contest, one of the nastiest in American history, became both a referendum and a revolution. Jackson crushed Adams in the electoral college by 178 to 83 and by a 56 percent to 44 percent margin in the popular vote. The total of over 1.1 million ballots, with Jackson receiving 650,000 votes and Adams garnering 500,000, tripled the number cast in 1824. John Quincy Adams, the president and his policies, had been decisively rejected. Certainly, Jackson's charismatic, if divisive, persona, military record, and superior political organization impacted the voters. Concurrently, his emphasis on cleansing Washington of corruption and restoring the values of the Founders resonated with Americans weary of a decade of scandal and feuds over patronage. Importantly, however, most white males had been granted the right to vote by their state constitutions before Jackson took office in 1829. His candidacy and the competitive two-party system of Jacksonian Democrats and National Republicans gave voice to an inspired American electorate. A new era of mass democracy had arisen, ushered in by a political configuration that would evolve and endure until destroyed by the contest over slavery on the eve of the Civil War.[30]

Notes

1 Marquis James, *The Life of Andrew Jackson* (New York: Bobbs–Merrill, 1938), 291–93.
2 Ibid., 293–96; Jackson, July 14, 1818, to A.J. Donelson, *Jackson Papers*, IV, 222; James Monroe, July 19, 1818, to Jackson, ibid., 224–27; Jackson, August 19, 1818, to Monroe, ibid., 236–38.
3 Jackson, November 15, 1818, to Monroe, ibid., 246–48; John H. Eaton, November 20, 1818, to Jackson, ibid., 248–49; James, *Andrew Jackson*, 297–301. The four defeated measures included

condemning Jackson for executing the British subjects, on executing them without presidential approval, on the seizure of Pensacola, and on drafting a law prohibiting the invasion of foreign territory without congressional approval. Robert Remini, *Andrew Jackson and the Course of American Empire, 1767–1821* (New York: Harper and Row, 1972), 374.

4   Jackson, September 17, 1819, to A.J. Donelson, *Jackson Papers*, IV, 322–23; Jackson, October 2, 1819, to Robert Y. Hayne, ibid., 333–34; Jackson, November 29, 1819, to Monroe, ibid., 342–43; Jackson, January 6, 1820, to John Clark, ibid., 349–50; Jackson, February 1, 1820, to George Gibson, ibid., 355–56; Jackson, December 21, 1820, to Calhoun, ibid., 409–10; Jackson, February 6, 1819, to Rachel, ibid., 271.

5   John Niven, *John C. Calhoun and the Price of Union* (Baton Rouge: Louisiana State University Press, 1988), 71–75; Irving Bartlett, *John C. Calhoun,* (New York: W.W. Norton, 1993), 95–98; Jackson, October 30, 1818, to Monroe, *Jackson Papers*, IV, 245–46.

6   Rachel Jackson, October 19, 1818, to AJ Donelson, ibid., 244–45; Jackson, February 24, 1817, to A.J. Donelson, ibid., 91–92; Jackson, April 26, 1822, to A.J. Donelson, ibid., V, 176–77.

7   Jackson, January 1, 1821, to James Monroe, ibid., V, 3–4; July 26, 1822, ibid., 207–08; Jackson, July 25, 1822, to A.J. Donelson, ibid., 205–06.

8   James Monroe, January 24, 1821, to Jackson, ibid., 9; Jackson, February 11, 1821, to Monroe, ibid., 10; Jackson, March 31, 1821, to A.J. Donelson, ibid., 24–25; Jackson, March 1, April 11, 1821, to John Coffee, ibid., 14–15, 27–28.

9   Jackson, April 30, 1821, to José Maria Callava, ibid., 33–34; J. Bronaugh and H. Brackenridge, May 7, 1821, to Jackson, ibid., 36–37.

10 Rachel Jackson, July 23, 1821, to Elizabeth Kingsley, ibid., 79–82; Jackson, July 29, 1821, to John C. Calhoun, ibid., 86–87; A. Jackson, August 2, 1821, to James Jackson, ibid., 91–92.

11 Jackson, August 22, 1821, to R. Butler and J. Bronaugh, ibid., 94–96.

12 Samuel Overton, August 1, 1821, to A. Jackson, ibid., 89–90; Jackson, January 29, 1822, to George Gibson, ibid., 139; Jackson, May 2, 1822, to James Gadsden, ibid., 179–81; Sam Houston, August 3, 1822, to Jackson, ibid., 211–12.

13 Jackson, June 29, 1822, to Richard K. Call, ibid., 197–99; Jackson, August 1, 1822, to James C. Bronaugh, ibid., 210–11; Jackson, June 29, 1822, to John Hamblen, ibid., 200.

14 John Eaton, January 11, 1823, to Jackson, ibid., 235–38; Jackson, February 19, 1823, to Monroe, ibid., 251–52; Jackson, March 10, 1823, to John Coffee, ibid., 257–58; Jackson, March 24, 1823, to Edward Livingston, ibid., 264–65.

15 Jackson, January 13, June 2, November 10, 1823, to Anthony W. Butler, ibid.

16 Jackson, August 12, 1823, to John C. Calhoun, ibid., 287–88.

17 Ibid., Jackson, December 7, 1823, to William B. Lewis, ibid., 323–24.

18 Jackson Papers, V, 294–97; Jackson, October 4, 1823, to J.C. Calhoun, ibid., 300–02; Jackson, October 5, October 24, 1823, to John Coffee, ibid., 302–03, 309–10.

19 Jackson, November 8, 1823, to John Overton, ibid., 316; Jackson, December 7, 1823, to Rachel, ibid., 322–23.

20 Jackson, December 21, 1823, to William S. Fulton, ibid., 328–29; Jackson, January 2, 1824, to G.W. Martin, ibid., 334.

21 Jackson, January 21, 1824, to A.J. Donelson, ibid., 343–44; Jackson, February 6, 1824, to Rachel Jackson, ibid., 351–52; Jackson, February 15, 1824, to John Coffee, ibid., 357–58; Jackson, February 26, 1824, to A.J. Donelson, ibid., 366–67.

22 Jackson, May 20, 1824, to Henry Baldwin, ibid., 411–12; Robert V. Remini, *Andrew Jackson and the Course of American Freedom, 1822–1832* (New York: Harper and Row, 1981), 59–73; Sharon Ann Murphy, "The Myth and Reality of Andrew Jackson's Rise in the Election of 1824," in Sean Patrick Adams, *A Companion to the Era of Andrew Jackson* (Malden, MA: Blackwell, 2014), 260–78.

23 Jackson, August 13, 1824, to George Wilson, ibid., 433–34; John M. Sacher, "The Elections of 1824 and 1828 and the Birth of Modern Politics," in Adams, *Companion,* 280–84; Mark R. Cheatham, *Southerner* (Baton Rouge: Louisiana State University Press, 2013), 99–104.

24 Jackson, December 19, 1824, to John Overton, *Jackson Papers,* V, 455; Jackson, December 27, 1824, to John Coffee, ibid., 457–58; Rachel Jackson, December 23, 1824, to Elizabeth Kingsley, ibid., 456–57; Remini, *American Freedom,* 80–84.
25 Remini, *American Freedom,* 84–99; Jackson, January 29, February 14, 1825, to William B. Lewis, *Jackson Papers,* VI, 22–23, 29–30; Sacher, "Elections of 1824 and 1828," 284–86.
26 Jackson, March 3, 1826, to John Branch, ibid., 141–43; Jackson, July 29, 1826, to John D. Terrell, ibid., 192; Jackson, October 5, 1826, to John Coffee, ibid., 226–27; Jackson, May 3, 1826, to James K. Polk, ibid., 166–67; Jackson, June 29, 1828, to James Hamilton, ibid., 476–77. Sacher, "Elections of 1824 and 1828," 290–92.
27 *Jackson Papers,* VI, 344, fnte 2; Robert Remini, *The Election of Andrew Jackson* (Philadelphia: J.B. Lippincott, 1963), 153.
28 Remini, *The Election of Andrew Jackson* (Philadelphia: J.B. Lippincott, 1963), 102–05, 117–18; Sacher, "Elections of 1824 and 1828," 288–91.
29 Cheathem, *Southerner,* 86.
30 Remini, *Election of Jackson,* 183–91.

CHAPTER **4**

THE WHITE HOUSE YEARS

FIRST TERM (1829–1833)

Andrew and Rachel had been vindicated. In spite of the slander and accusations, some of which, sadly, were true, the people overwhelmingly chose him as the seventh president of the United States. The triumph was short-lived. Rachel persisted in a melancholy state following the death of Lyncoya in the late spring of 1828. The nasty tone of the campaign provided added stress, as she heard the charges against her husband aired in public forums.

While reluctantly preparing to travel to Washington, where she would no doubt face the gossip and whispers of her husband's enemies, Rachel stumbled across campaign literature that revealed the depth of the mean-spiritedness hurled at the Jacksons. Her reputation and virtue had been at the forefront of the National Republican onslaught. Rachel's health had not been good, and minimal exercise exhausted her, leaving her breathless. The raven-haired beauty Jackson wed more than three decades before had become a pipe-smoking, coarse-looking, stout old lady whom a visitor noted could easily be confused with a washerwoman. Now her emotional state teetered on collapse. The couple considered the possibility of Rachel temporarily remaining in Nashville, at least until after the pressure of the inaugural crowds had dissipated. Both yielded, however, to public expectations and prepared to depart for the capital.

On December 18, Rachel experienced intense pain in her left arm and chest, and collapsed into the arms of her slave, Hannah. She had suffered a serious heart attack. The doctors rushed to the Hermitage, bleeding her several times to help relieve the agony. Rachel spent the next four days in bed and an anguished Jackson believed that the crisis had passed. On the night of December 22, however, he was awakened by the desperate cries of the slaves; his wife had suffered a second attack. This time it proved fatal. Distraught and inconsolable, Andrew buried Rachel in the garden at the

Hermitage, wondering how he could continue on his presidential voyage without her by his side. She had been a loyal and loving companion, steadfastly enduring his frequent absences and tolerating his ambitions and adventures. Quite possibly, the months of separation prompted by her husband's military and political service contributed to her depressed mental state and physical deterioration. Jackson thought, however, that the vile nature of the recent White House campaign had led to her demoralization, and then her death. "I can forgive all who have wronged me," he solemnly told friends at her funeral, "but will have fervently to pray that I may have grace to enable me to forget or forgive any enemy who has ever maligned that blessed one who is now safe from all suffering and sorrow, whom they tried to put to shame for my sake." Jackson knew who had killed his wife, and, true to his word, he would never forgive or forget.[1]

At the moment of his greatest victory, Andrew Jackson suffered his deepest despair. Weeks passed, the gloom enveloping the Hermitage periodically broken by the squawking of "Poll," the African grey parrot that Jackson bought for Rachel in 1827. The beloved bird became a living remembrance of her. Jackson left "Poll" behind in Nashville, but reminded a family member of the importance of the creature's care, "I value this bird more than anything my dear wife left—she thought so much of it."

After almost a month of brooding and prayer, he could no longer delay his departure. The president-elect made the three-week journey to his inaugural by steamboat to Pittsburgh, then via the Cumberland Road (the funding of which he had once opposed), arriving on February 11 in Washington, DC. Along the way, he received a preview of what was to come in the capital, crowds of enthusiastic common folk crushing to greet him and shake his hand. The mourning Jackson, clad in black suit and tie, accommodated his supporters, but avoided any discussion of public matters, especially the composition of his new cabinet. He decided not to call on the president, and Adams, in turn, refused to attend the inauguration. The political polarization had begun.[2]

A New Administration

Regardless, a beautiful inaugural day, March 4, offered the huge throng of 20,000 assembled the consummate moment to acclaim their hero. After witnessing the oath of office administered by Chief Justice John Marshall at the Capitol, the masses rushed to congratulate the president. When he moved to the reception at the White House, they followed, streaming down Pennsylvania Avenue. The planned genteel gathering turned chaotic as the crowd (black and white, male and female, and city and country) decided that this was their party. In the ensuing near-riot, liquor spilled, glasses shattered, and men in muddy boots trampled over the furniture. The polite classes of Washington stood by in shock and despair as the horde took control of this traditionally proper affair. The White House became so packed and the multitude so enthused about saluting Jackson that he was escorted back to Gadsby's Hotel for his own safety. "The majesty of the people had disappeared," Washington socialite Margaret Bayard Smith lamented. This indeed was the mobocracy that many feared. Old Hickory frequently voiced his confidence in the principle of mass democracy, the will of the people and majority rule, not a representative republic in which ideas and policies were funneled through leaders produced by legislative bodies. The popular voice in government and a changing social scene now seemed much closer to reality.[3]

While Jackson offered only a vague program of reform in his brief March inaugural, he assumed a more aggressive posture in his lengthy first message to Congress, delivered on December 8, 1829. Countering the strident nationalistic policies of Adams, the new chief executive sought to scale down the size and scope of the federal government, reduce expenditures, and pay off the national debt. He consistently urged a moderate and "just" tariff, which would raise revenue to help fund that debt, while endorsing the limited use of federal monies for internal improvements. At the same time, he promised to cleanse the capital's political stables of filth and corruption.

For Jackson, corruption involved more than the misuse or stealing of public money; it included ambitious actions or favoritism in policies, contracts, or appointments that advanced the interests of the select few over the many. Such political selfishness destroyed the very roots of the democracy and violated the nation's fundamental precepts of morality, individual liberty, and responsibility. During the Monroe administration, the general witnessed investigations into such misdeeds firsthand in Washington, and was kept informed about others. Secretaries Calhoun and Crawford sought, with considerable success, to embarrass each other and derail their respective presidential campaigns by poisoning the political pot. Congressional inquiries into fraud, embezzlement, and boondoggles under Calhoun and Crawford involved contractors, land companies, customs houses, and banks. While neither man appeared to gain personal wealth, certainly friends and supporters did so. Importantly, and to Jackson's great irritation, Crawford not only survived these challenges to his reputation, he became the frontrunner in the ill-fated caucus for the White House in 1824.

Convinced that corruption at levels large and small remained problematic throughout the federal government, Jackson made it a priority to root out the evil. In 1829, Amos Kendall spearheaded investigations by the administration, especially into the Treasury, which uncovered miscreants in land sales and customs who had abused public monies. These revelations and subsequent removals from office, though not unusually large or different in number from other administrations, caught the public's attention and convinced the president of the rightness of his cause. For him, the rite of purification meant a reduction in the number of officeholders as well as the removal of wrongdoers from their posts.

In turn, Jackson encountered his own share of censure for corruption based on favoritism in public appointments—the so-called "spoils system." Critics argue that he founded the system in which capable public officeholders were replaced by loyal supporters, regardless of their talent. In reality, Jackson removed only about 10 percent of the some 11,500 federal employees during his two terms in office. The figure is similar to the percentage of Federalists that Thomas Jefferson dismissed when his Democratic–Republican party assumed power in 1801 with only 3,000 employees. What struck contemporaries and scholars alike was the dramatic and public nature of Jackson's initial removals.

Corruption could be cured by rotation in office and limited four-year appointments, the president argued in his first message to Congress. "Offices were not established to give support to particular men at the public expense." In spite of such bold statements and apparent good intentions to name honorable and honest men to office, Jackson made his own share of poor appointments. Notably, Samuel Swartwout, the Collector of the Port of New York, fled the country after skimming off $1 million in government funds. More broadly, Old Hickory established a rewards system that was indeed based on political loyalty and deeply flawed. Predictably, succeeding administrations embraced the concept with growing affection.

Jackson firmly believed that majority rule and greater involvement by the people would purify the political process. Reflecting upon his own disappointments in 1824–1825, he urged that the popular vote replace the electoral college in the selection process, and that presidents serve only one four- to six-year term in office. Similarly, senators and judges should be elected by the people, not chosen by state legislatures or appointed. While Congress enacted none of these reforms, Jackson's declarations further clarified his principles and priorities.[4]

The president's cabinet constituted an important base for both counsel and political support. Traditionally, the men chosen represented the party faithful from wide-ranging sections of the country. Jackson added another layer to the qualifications for office: he demanded loyalty and support for his agenda. Those who disagreed must resign. The cabinet he picked proved to be a major disappointment, and the departures came sooner than expected. While most Americans were unfamiliar with the new members, the president attempted to geographically balance his advisors, while rewarding their support. Secretary of State Martin Van Buren, former senator and newly governor of New York, was the strongest appointment. The remaining selections—Samuel Ingham of Pennsylvania in the Treasury, John Branch of North Carolina in the Navy, John Berrien of Georgia as Attorney General, and William Barry of Kentucky as Postmaster General—were, at best, mediocre. While men of considerable public service, they were neither skilled administrators nor particularly knowledgeable about their departments. Historians have generally considered this initial Jackson cabinet among the weakest of the nineteenth century. The president must bear the responsibility for his choices. While he controlled his reform agenda, their competency and cooperation, or lack thereof, would help determine its fate.[5]

The Petticoat Affair

Perhaps the worst of the appointments was his close personal friend and fellow Tennessean, Secretary of War John Eaton. After the loss of Rachel, it is easy to comprehend why Jackson wanted comrades close by, and his relationship with Eaton, whom the general regarded as almost a son, reached back more than a decade. The problem with Eaton had little to do with the War Department and much to do with his choice of women. In January 1829, Eaton, a 38-year-old widower, had married the younger Margaret O'Neale Timberlake. Margaret, the daughter of a Washington hotel owner, was beautiful, vivacious, and outspoken. She had worked at her father's establishment, the Franklin Hotel, where Jackson had resided in 1824. Even though she married at sixteen to U.S. Navy purser John Timberlake in 1816, and had three children, Margaret still received the attention of numerous smitten politicians. Timberlake struggled financially, and, in 1828, committed suicide while on an extended sea voyage. The decorum of the era dictated that she grieve his death for at least a year. Instead, she and John Eaton decided to wed within six months. The rumors flew in proper capital society, including the contention that John and Margaret had sexual relations, and that she had miscarried his child. Jackson, with the memory of Rachel fresh in his mind, personally felt the arrows of such gossip, and encouraged the exchanging of vows as quickly as possible.[6]

Jackson's vision of building a community within his administration evaporated around the ensuing Eaton scandal. Refined Washington ladies, led by Vice President Calhoun's wife, Floride, refused to call upon Margaret, and the cabinet wives only grudgingly attended a November dinner at the White House. Thereafter, the wives were pointedly absent from functions where the Eatons might appear. Even more hurtful to Jackson, Emily Donelson, the young wife of his nephew Andrew Jackson Donelson, and de facto hostess at the mansion, joined the other women in snubbing Margaret.

The president took this social breakdown in his inner circle very seriously. As a paternalistic southern gentleman, he stressed the protection of female honor and the required loyalty of extended family to his will. His decision to include the Eatons within that family should not be challenged. Only Secretaries Van Buren and Barry seemed sympathetic and supportive. When it became apparent that the cabinet was socially dysfunctional, Jackson tried his best to restore order and harmony.[7]

A September 1829 cabinet meeting to discuss the dilemma, attended by several concerned clergymen, quickly turned acrimonious. The president, in defense of Margaret's honor, shouted at one minister, "She is as chaste as a virgin." There seemed little ground for calm discussion of her virtue or arriving at a solution for the quandary. Clearly, Jackson would have been best served by recognizing the oncoming storm that Eaton's appointment caused and finding a political or diplomatic slot for him outside of the capital. A compromise allowing his old friend to depart the administration gracefully for another post might have salvaged the situation. Jackson did not think in such terms. A challenge had been issued; the president would not yield.[8]

Old Hickory had allowed petticoats to interfere with politics. As the months passed, the situation worsened to the point where he exiled both Emily and A. J. Donelson to Nashville as punishment for their recalcitrant behavior. Margaret did little to help the situation, continuing to act and speak in a brazen manner that offered no chance of endearing her to the Washington establishment. Reluctant to hold the Eatons or himself responsible for the difficulties, Jackson blamed first Henry Clay and then John C. Calhoun. The president determined that the commotion was part of a larger plan to disrupt his administration. The social war raged within the government, affecting matters of trust and communication, until April 1831, when Jackson reached a breaking point. Frustrated and angry, he asked for and received the resignation of virtually the entire cabinet.[9]

The action stunned the nation, which had been largely ignorant of the imbroglio over Margaret. The cabinet was viewed as an integral part of the executive branch, a body of trusted counselors with varying views, and a place for conciliation. No president had ever had the audacity to dismiss his whole body of advisors. Loyalty to the chief executive became the new litmus test. It was a dramatic exercise of presidential power. Some members survived. Van Buren returned as vice president in 1832 and Barry continued as postmaster general. Eaton went on to serve as governor of Florida and minister to Spain. Even so, the scandal proved to be an unnecessary and destructive embarrassment to an administration that had entered Washington with such great promise of hope and change.

The "petticoat affair" had its clear winners and losers. Some 150 years ago in his multi-volume biography of Jackson, historian James Parton posited the notion that "the political history of the United States, for the last thirty years, dates from the moment when the soft hand of Mr. Van Buren touched Mrs. Eaton's knocker." Van Buren, a widower with remarkable social skills, had done his utmost to ingratiate himself with the Eatons—whether that involved a brush with her breast, however, is debatable. For whatever reason, his support of Margaret served him well, and his stock rose accordingly with the president.[10]

The Split with Calhoun

In contrast, Vice President Calhoun found himself in a downward political spiral. The attitude of John and Floride towards the Eatons was the culmination of a growing separation between Calhoun and Jackson. The issues were threefold. First, in 1828, Calhoun had written *The South Carolina Exposition and Protest*, a document penned in response to the high rates proposed in the recent Tariff of Abominations. Calhoun's tract argued for the primacy of states' rights, fearing a tyranny of the majority that might express itself through the federal government. He saw the tariff as an unconstitutional measure to tax some states at the expense of others. The aggrieved states had a right, Calhoun maintained, to elect conventions to nullify a federal law that worked against the best interests of their citizens. He drafted the *Protest* anonymously, but many people, including Jackson, suspected the identity of the author.

While also a champion of states' rights, the president could not have disagreed more strongly with the notion of nullification. Such an extreme doctrine threatened the effectiveness, perhaps even the permanence, of the Union. These real differences became public on April 13, 1830, at the dinner celebration of Thomas Jefferson's birthday. Jackson stood and pointedly delivered the toast, "Our federal union, it must be preserved." Calhoun responded with an equally strong and defiant voice, "Our federal union—next to our liberty most dear."[11]

Second, the tariff itself separated Calhoun and Jackson. Following the War of 1812, the South Carolinian had been part of a coterie of young Democratic-Republicans who endorsed a nationalist economic system, including the protective Tariff of 1816. As his state evolved over the decade and assumed a more clamorous states' rights posture, Calhoun wisely adjusted so as to remain politically viable. Hence, he expressed a strong opposition to protective duties that might harm the export of southern cotton to Europe. Jackson, in contrast, had consistently argued for more moderate rates and mutual sacrifice by each section of the country.

Third, Jackson confirmed an earlier suspicion regarding Calhoun's support of the general's actions in the Florida incursion of 1818. For years,

Jackson believed that in the heated cabinet discussions that ensued, Secretary of War Calhoun had joined Secretary of State Adams in backing him. That assumption had contributed to the growing amity between Jackson and Calhoun, allowing the Carolinian to make the most unusual transition of serving as vice president under Adams to holding the same office under Jackson. In 1828, Jackson learned that Calhoun might indeed have joined Clay in criticizing him for the Seminole campaign. The president did not act, however, until he had received a letter from old enemy William H. Crawford in May 1830, detailing the extent of Calhoun's hostility. An exchange of correspondence between Jackson and the Carolinian resulted. Jackson challenged Calhoun's loyalty and the vice president's feeble and ineffective response only convinced the president that he had been deceived. Old Hickory may well have loosely interpreted, or even violated, his instructions from President Monroe and Secretary Calhoun in the Seminole War, a viewpoint Calhoun honestly expressed during their cabinet meetings. For Jackson, however, the deception arose from allowing him to believe for more than a decade that he had both the Carolinian's friendship and support in a time of personal and professional crisis.

In 1831, sensing the extent of the damage, Calhoun published a 52-page public explanation of his actions in the *U.S. Telegraph*. The lengthy discourse may have satisfied his supporters, but did nothing to change Jackson's mind. Old Hickory had determined that Calhoun, his quondam friend, was an ambitious "villain" who conspired against the Eatons, his presidency, and even the permanence of the Union. Calhoun's role in the administration had come to an end. He would ultimately resign his position in December 1832, returning a few months later to haunt Jackson in the U.S. Senate.[12]

The separation with Calhoun was an ominous sign for the new Democratic Party. Jackson had now alienated several members of his former cabinet and the vice president, key individuals in maintaining southern support for the upcoming election in 1832. The president did his best to demonstrate his commitment to states' right principles, an issue important to many in that section of the country. In May 1830, he vetoed a congressional measure providing for an extension of the National Road in Kentucky between Maysville and Lexington. Jackson likely took genuine delight in the decision, since that particular stretch of highway included Henry Clay's old congressional district. The president supported funding of roads and canals, but determined that spending federal money for a project entirely within a state to be unconstitutional. Not only would such measures drive the government further into debt, but the local undertaking should be paid for solely by the citizens of Kentucky. Jackson came to believe that this nettlesome question needed to be resolved by a constitutional amendment.

While the veto angered many westerners, it was a step towards reassuring his southern followers by both symbolic gesture and practical action of his conservative, strict constructionist views of the Constitution.[13]

Indian Removal

Indian removal gave Jackson another opportunity to demonstrate his commitment not only to states' rights, but also to national security and the progress of white farmers in both North and South. Compelling Native Americans to give up their lands by a variety of means fair and foul had been government policy since the days of Thomas Jefferson. The Sage of Monticello embraced the rather unsavory notion of deliberately getting the Indians into debt through trade, then seizing their territory when they could not pay the amount owed. Jefferson viewed the Indians as a race that showed promise, and might be "civilized" through assimilation, white contact, and education. Should that strategy fail, however, removal seemed a reasonable alternative.

After the defeat of both the Creeks in the South and Tecumseh's confederacy of tribes in the North during the War of 1812, large scale armed Indian resistance east of the Mississippi River ended. Smaller struggles, such as the tragic Black Hawk War of 1832, proved disastrous for the Sauk and Mesquakie Indians who tried to return from Iowa to their native lands in Illinois. In Florida, the Seminoles engaged in a more elusive conflict, fighting a lengthy and imaginative guerrilla campaign (1835–1842). The Second Seminole War, which resulted in the capture and death of Chief Osceola, the burning of Indian villages, impending starvation, and eventual capitulation, proved immensely unpopular among many white Americans. While the Seminoles refused to formally surrender, by the end of 1842 the substantial majority of the nation had been removed from Tampa to Oklahoma. Only a few hundred remained to fight yet a Third Seminole War (1855–1858) that resulted in additional forced evacuation to the West.

The aforementioned removal strategy developed by Secretary of War Calhoun in 1818 met with disappointing results from a white perspective. The policy seemed fair enough: offer the Indians lands west of the Mississippi in exchange for their lands east of the river. Their travel would be compensated by the government, and start-up funds made available to aid in the transition to their new homes. Jackson, one of the commissioners who negotiated with the southern tribes, firmly endorsed the exchange as best for both white progress and Indian survival. Although a flurry of agreements resulted from the talks, the Indians in the South generally proved reluctant to move west. With few exceptions, they stalled, negotiated new treaties, and managed to delay their departure through the decade of the

1820s. Accordingly, the patience of white settlers with both the Indians and federal government grew increasingly thin.[14]

Thus, when Jackson came into office in 1829, he made relocating the Indians a priority. Pressured by the White House, in May 1830, Congress, by a very narrow margin (102 to 97 in the House), passed a Removal Act that accelerated the process. Although the Democrats controlled Congress, the measure encountered particularly heavy fire from northeastern National Republicans who passionately argued the immorality of removal and recoiled at the president's meddling. His hand in the legislation smacked too much of the old military chieftain interfering in the legislative agenda. Division within the Democratic ranks also made the vote close. The anticipated veto of the Maysville Road angered a number of Jacksonians in Pennsylvania and Ohio, who manifested their displeasure by deserting Old Hickory on the Indian question.

The matter rapidly became intensely partisan, serving as fodder for the 1832 campaign. The law itself did not compel the Indians to leave their tribal lands, but it removed any federal protection against white encroachment. Those Indians who remained were under the tender care of the states and their soil-hungry farmers. The ultimate cost of removal was high in money, land, and lives. During the decades of the 1820s and 1830s, approximately 100,000 Indians, North and South, would be marched or transported from their homelands. Under Jackson, more than seventy treaties were negotiated at a cost of $68 million, with the Indians receiving 32 million acres west of the Mississippi. In return, they agreed to surrender 100 million acres east of the river.

Since most Indians did not depart willingly, the inevitable conflict of cultures occurred, threatening the fragile peace along the frontier. The Cherokee, some 20,000 strong, strove to meet Anglo expectations, establishing a written language, constitution, and even a police force. Living in log cabins and farming the land, they were in many ways almost indistinguishable from their white yeoman counterparts. The Cherokee, who owned more than 1,500 African Americans by 1830, joined the other southern tribes in adopting slavery. Still, their race and their land ownership compelled the Indians' departure. The Cherokee did not simply drag their feet, they took their case to the U.S. Supreme Court in 1831 (*Cherokee Nation v. Georgia*) and 1832 (*Worcester v. Georgia*). The Indians based their argument on their sovereignty as an independent nation with whom the U.S. government had negotiated treaties. The court rejected the contention of an "independent" entity, substituting "dependent" instead. This partial victory indicated that the Cherokee, while not immune from oversight by the U.S. government, were not obliged to follow the laws or suffer interference from the states in which they resided.

The ruling had given the Indians hope, but no protection. An aroused Andrew Jackson supposedly responded, "John Marshall has made his decision, now let him enforce it." While the president never uttered this statement, he had no intention of acting on a legal decision that would help maintain the Indians on their eastern lands. Missionary Samuel Worcester, who had been arrested by Georgia officials for ministering to the Indians without a license, was pardoned by Governor Wilson Lumpkin on the condition that he leave the state. Worcester wisely did so, eventually moving to Oklahoma to continue his ministry among the Indians.

In December 1835, the Cherokee were pressured to negotiate yet another agreement. The Treaty of New Echota provided for the cession of tribal holdings in the Southeast in exchange for compensation and western lands. The pact mirrored the sharp division within the Cherokee between the minority "Treaty Party," led by John Ridge, who believed that removal and bargaining to best advantage with the whites was the only realistic course, versus the majority "National Party," guided by John Ross, who hoped to remain on their eastern lands indefinitely. Not surprisingly, Jackson applauded the Ridge faction's wisdom in approving the New Echota accord. The Senate duly acknowledged Ross's fervent objections in March 1836, but still passed the treaty by one vote. To worsen matters for the Cherokee, gold had been discovered near Dahlonega in north Georgia in 1828. Prospectors possessed with gold fever now joined land hungry settlers, as thousands rushed into Indian lands over the next decade. The odds of the Indians holding on dwindled with each passing year.

Many northern tribes had already moved west. Beginning in 1830, with the Choctaws, southern tribes large (Cherokee) and small (Seminole) ceded their lands. Most commenced the sojourn across the Mississippi. They had little choice. Even had Jackson agreed to defend them, and he did not, the federal government lacked the capacity to protect tens of thousands of Indians covering a vast territory. A nation with no immediate military threat had little need for a large standing army. Consequently, U.S. forces had been scattered during Calhoun's tenure in the War Department and drastically reduced to a few thousand men. The country fought its battles with short-term volunteers and state militias. Since the southern militias were largely composed of farmers, activating Alabama units to shield the Creeks against those same farmers had little chance of success. Likewise, the prospect of Vermont volunteers or the Massachusetts militia called into duty to safeguard Indians in Georgia seemed doomed to fail. Indeed, given rising sectional tensions in the South, such a maneuver could have hastened the Civil War by thirty years. Many still seethed over the high protective tariff of 1828, and South Carolina began to grouse about nullification. In 1832, that state stayed isolated in its extreme position on the tariff, but some southerners expressed their sympathy. Could an aggressive stance by the Jackson administration in defense of the Indians have pushed other states into South Carolina's camp?

The inability, much less the unwillingness, of the federal government to defend the Indians and the possibility of sectional strife does not excuse the racism and greed involved in forcing the natives from their lands. The immorality of the policy played out in dislocation and death over the decade. Of the almost 50,000 southern Indians that traveled west by land and water, the most horrific journey was the infamous "Trail of Tears." The 1,000-mile trek from eastern Tennessee to Oklahoma resulted in the demise of over 4,000 of the 13,000 deported Cherokees. Ironically, this tragedy occurred in 1838 under the presidency of Martin Van Buren. Perhaps if Jackson the general had been in command, he would have engineered a more energetic and efficient removal process, thus averting the Trail of Tears. Sadly, it seems unlikely. Prior removals, commencing with the Choctaw, reveal similar disasters.

Poor planning by the U.S. army and the greed and inefficiency of private contractors provided the human element. Nature contributed brutally cold weather and rampant disease to produce needless starvation and death. The removal policy was longstanding, and Old Hickory must share in the responsibility, since he both approved and enforced its application. While voices of dissent could be heard in the Northeast, the American people largely endorsed the plan which made valuable land available for cotton and grain. Removal may have been racist and immoral, but those on the frontier rationalized the strategy and saw few alternatives.[15]

Election of 1832

As the presidential election approached, the various political contingents scrambled to choose their candidates. Following the caucus fiasco of 1824, the two nascent parties had sorted their problems out at the state level in 1828. With popular democracy on the rise in 1832, three parties held national conventions in Baltimore to pick their nominees. In an interesting twist, the Anti-Masonic Party, formed in the 1820s to eliminate the perceived threat of the Masonic Order to American democracy, held the first such meeting in September 1831. The delegates chose former Attorney General William Wirt as their nominee. In December, the National Republicans predictably selected Henry Clay. Since Jackson supported the concept of a national conclave, over 300 delegates representing all the states (except Missouri) assembled in Baltimore from May 21–23 to "concur" on the nomination of Old Hickory for a second term. While noteworthy as a pioneering gathering, the Democratic sessions produced little drama.

The only controversy swirled around Jackson's choice of Martin Van Buren as vice president. He had worked his way into the inner circle of the White House, taking advantage of regular morning horseback rides with Jackson to promote both his ideas and place as the general's successor. This position was strengthened in January 1832 by the Senate's refusal to confirm Van Buren's nomination as Minister to England. The tie-breaking negative vote was cast by a gleeful Vice President John C. Calhoun. A furious Jackson responded, "By the Eternal! I'll smash them!" Van Buren, dubbed "The Little Magician" for his political skills, had alienated as many Democrats as he had befriended during his time in the capital. While the Baltimore delegates debated the alternatives to the slick New Yorker, they eventually yielded to Jackson's preference.[16]

Jackson was in a weakened state, physically and politically. Now sixty-five, the president endured extended and enervating battles with the flu and poorly fitting false teeth that rubbed his gums raw. More painful, the ball from the Benton brawl of 1813 had traversed down his left inner arm and lodged near the skin. Since Jackson could feel and move the ball, his family urged that it be removed. In January 1832, a visit to a Philadelphia physician resulted in the doctor cutting and excising the bullet—without the use of anesthetic. While his physical body soon healed, Jackson realized the damage to his political body, the Democrats, was much more severe. The divisions within the party, compounded with the rise of the Anti-Masons, especially in the Northeast, and the popularity of Clay, posed real obstacles to his re-election. Jackson was a Mason, which might cost him vital support in New York and Pennsylvania, but fortunately so was Clay. Each section had reason to become disaffected with the president: Indian removal in New England, the Maysville Road veto in the West, and the splintering with Calhoun and the cabinet in the South.[17]

The National Republicans seized the moment, criticizing the Democrats' Indian policy, and endorsing Clay's "American System" of federally funded internal improvements. Focusing upon the abuses heaped upon the Cherokee, the party platform made clear that Jackson had allowed Georgia to violate federal treaties with impunity. To reinforce the point, their delegates nominated a volunteer counsel for the Cherokee before the Supreme Court, John Sergeant of Pennsylvania, as vice president. Clay and his compatriots also recognized that Jackson was vulnerable on altering the high protective tariff and re-chartering the Bank of the United States. Either could be the final nail in Old Hickory's political coffin.[18]

The Tariff Question

By the 1820s, the tariff had become a sectionally divisive problem. Since the federal government could tax imports under the Constitution, the first

Secretary of the Treasury, Alexander Hamilton, viewed the tariff as a revenue measure, serving to fund federal obligations and pay off loans from foreign countries. The rise of American industry, particularly in the Northeast during the era of the War of 1812, added a second dimension to the tariff—a way to protect U.S. manufacturers from foreign competition by taxing imports at a significant level. After years of blockades and embargoes, in 1815, the British began to dump their products, especially cheap textiles and iron goods, on the American market. Congressional Democratic-Republicans responded with the first protective measure the following year. Averaging a modest 20 percent in rates, the bill surprisingly garnered support from all sections of the country. Following the financial Panic of 1819, the pressure for further protection resulted in 1824 in a new tariff (which Senator Jackson approved), raising the duties to about 30 percent. Southerners opposed the legislation, reasonably asking whether such increases would work against them. Would they have to pay more for manufactured goods imported into the South, and would the Europeans retaliate with their own duties on items such as cotton or tobacco?

The genesis of the 1828 "Tariff of Abominations" (and its 45 percent rate) seemed as much about politics as economics. Anticipating the November presidential contest, the Jacksonians felt secure about holding the South, while conceding New England to the Adams forces. The band of states from New York and Pennsylvania into the Midwest and Upper South (Ohio, Indiana, Illinois, Missouri, and Kentucky) would be the battleground. The Democrats, who controlled Congress, developed a strategy to give those states protective duties on items essential to their local economies, from hemp and molasses to wool and iron.

Satisfying those interests, while garnering enough support for passage from potentially hostile forces in Congress, however, required a master hand. Van Buren, the Magician, worked his spell, crafting a tariff measure which neither met the extreme desires of free trade southerners nor protectionist Yankees, but fell deftly onto the middle ground. With his leadership in the Senate and aided by fellow New Yorker Silas Wright, Jr. in the House, the Jacksonians packaged a balanced measure that seemed to offer something to almost everyone, although ultimately more to agricultural than manufacturing interests. Even so, last-minute concessions to the Northeast to increase the duties on imported woolens were needed to ensure success. In May, the measure passed the Senate by the narrow vote of 26 to 21.

The maneuver worked as planned in November. Old Hickory took a majority of the electoral votes in New York, and swept the remaining targeted states, as he cruised to victory. Furious southerners railed against the new tariff, Calhoun expressing the thoughts of many in his *Exposition and Protest*. Jackson was well aware of the hostility engendered by the bill, and attempted to calm the waters as early as June 1828. He assured South Carolina skeptic James Hamilton, Jr., that he was troubled by the "strong feelings of political excitement" the tariff had produced throughout the nation. While not openly endorsing the legislation, Jackson assured Hamilton that he championed "a judicious tariff," one that would be decided upon with "great calmness and due deliberation, with an eye to the prosperity of the whole Union." The general spoke of the United States as "one great family," and of the need for mutual concessions and equal benefits. Whether the new tariff measure would benefit or burden each section equally, he pondered, "can only be tested by experience." While Jackson waffled in his correspondence, calculating Democrats soon realized that the prize had been won, and some compromise must be made on the duties before the 1832 election. Jackson himself had little difficulty rationalizing a decrease. He saw the tariff primarily as a vehicle for raising money to pay the national debt. Since that day of fiscal solvency was fast approaching, he would later recommend a rapid reduction of rates to 27 percent.

Congress had its own ideas. In a three-day speech to the Senate, Clay, representative of the West and of his beliefs in supporting American industry, railed against any cutback, while southerners demanded dropping the duties lower than Jackson proposed. On July 9, after two months of lobbying and negotiation, Congress passed an equitable compromise that dropped the rates to 25 percent, but kept them high on iron, woolens, and cotton. Jackson reasoned that he had done his part, and that the measure would ultimately prove satisfactory to Americans in all sections of the country. At the same time, he remained concerned that the perpetually mischievous Calhoun would continue to engineer "a great noise." "The good sense of the people will put it down," he declared to his comrade John Coffee. In this case, Jackson misjudged both Calhoun and the citizens of South Carolina.[19]

The Bank War

The Bank of the United States posed a second headache. Headquartered in Philadelphia, the Second BUS had been chartered in 1816 in the twilight of the James Madison presidency. Previous opponents of the First BUS (1791–1811), such as Thomas Jefferson, had criticized the institution as unconstitutional and potentially abusive of its role in domestic and international finances. The powerful bank could print currency, house government revenues, and determine loan and interest rates. The fiscal crisis that accompanied the War of 1812, however, convinced many skeptical Democratic-Republicans, including Madison, who also opposed the First BUS, and Clay of the need for a central agency. The Second Bank was a private-public partnership, capitalized at $35 million (versus $10 million for the First Bank) with 80 percent generated by private stockholders and 20 percent from government funds. When the Panic of 1819 rocked the economy, many farmers blamed the bank's easy lending policies for their problems. The Marshall Court stepped into the middle of the controversy in the 1819 case of *McCulloch v. Maryland*, ruling the BUS to be constitutional, and denying the prerogative of a state to tax the bank notes of a federally chartered institution. "The power to tax is the power to destroy," the chief justice contended.[20]

As the economy improved in the 1820s, the reputation of the BUS, under the guidance of Nicholas Biddle, who became its president in 1823, rose accordingly. In spite of its success, Jackson suspected the institution. His distrust reached back into the 1790s, and included a cynical view of paper money and of the constitutionality of the bank. Jackson viewed the BUS as a genuine threat to American liberty. Although state banks also existed, the wide contacts and immense wealth of the Second Bank gave it monopolistic powers, as well as the ability to influence politicians and elections. When charges of corruption and political favoritism emerged in the Lexington, Kentucky, and Portsmouth, New Hampshire, branches in 1829, Jackson could take satisfaction that the bank was awash with his enemies. Biddle responded, digging a deep political hole for himself by exonerating Jeremiah Mason, president of the Portsmouth branch, of all charges, and directing his re-election. In an ill-advised letter of September 15 to Secretary of the Treasury Ingham, Biddle emphasized that the bank's officers were not accountable to the government for their behavior or actions. Such arrogance was misplaced, even for a popular and successful businessman who managed a largely private corporation.[21]

Jackson did not respond well to a challenge to the administration's authority, especially when millions of dollars in government funds rested in the bank's vaults. One month later, Jackson and Biddle met at the White House. Biddle only gradually came to sense the president's lack of support, reinforced by his own actions and those of his officers. It remains improbable, however, that the banker could have convinced Jackson to support the BUS in its existing form. Jackson informed Biddle that he disagreed with John Marshall; the bank was indeed unconstitutional. In his annual message of December 1829, Old Hickory called attention to the need for greater oversight of the BUS and the public's money. As scholar Stephen Mihm re-emphasized, "the Bank concentrated too much power in too few hands."

Biddle had been sent an early warning. Even so, Jackson vacillated between alternatives. In his 1830 message to Congress, he suggested a federally run institution with no stockholders that would make no loans and simply pay the government's expenses. Within the year, he had opened his mind to re-chartering the existing bank under a modified measure that would give the government greater authority. Since the bank's charter did not expire until

1836, reform and resolution of the differences between Jackson and Biddle did not demand immediate attention. The president seemed willing to compromise and turn resolution of the matter over to Congress.[22]

Other issues—the "petticoat affair," Indians, internal improvements, and foreign affairs—demanded more of Jackson's time than the bank question. Since he appeared to be reducing the bank as a priority, Biddle would have been wise to adopt a similarly low profile. Instead, sniping continued in the press, as the Philadelphian felt the need to defend his institution against perceived attacks by the administration. He was cheered on in his resistance by Henry Clay, who saw the bank as an issue to be exploited in the upcoming election. The National Republicans convinced Biddle to move for a re-charter in 1832—four years before its expiration. They viewed the tactic as a "no-lose" proposition. If Jackson approved the measure, the National Republicans would take credit for the extension, and Biddle would have the security of firmly establishing his bank for an additional two decades. If Jackson vetoed, the opposition would blast him for destroying a popular institution that benefited the economy.[23]

What would the president do? A number of Democrats, caught in the middle, feared Jackson's course, and sympathized with the bank. The party had tentative control of both houses of Congress, but support from within their ranks splintered, allowing the re-charter to pass in early July 1832 by a vote of 28 to 20 in the Senate and 106 to 84 in the House. The BUS garnered its strongest backing in the Northeast and from National Republicans; the opposition came from Democrats in the South. Jackson clearly understood the motivation for the bill, and realized that Biddle had joined his enemies in a political war to the death. Just as in the Eaton Affair, Jackson conflated the attacks on him and the nation. The personal became the political. He did not flinch. When Martin Van Buren visited the White House days later, a determined Old Hickory quietly told him, "The Bank, Mr. Van Buren, is trying to kill me, but I will kill it!" The president referred to the BUS as a "monster," an octopus-like hydra that used its tentacles to squeeze liberty out of the American people.[24]

Jackson vetoed more pieces of Congressional legislation, twelve in all, than his predecessors *combined*. Perhaps none caused a greater uproar than the July 10 rejection of the BUS. The message was the handiwork of the president and several members of his advisory "Kitchen Cabinet," specifically Amos Kendall and Roger B. Taney. The missive pulled no punches, striking the bank at various levels: (a) it was unconstitutional in spite of the prior Supreme Court ruling of 1819, and the executive branch had an equal right to interpret the Constitution on such matters; (b) the rich and powerful controlled and benefitted from the success of the bank, particularly foreigners who held $8 million in BUS stock; (c) the bank was a monopoly that controlled the domestic and foreign currency and exchange rates; and (d) the BUS meddled with and interfered in American elections, undermining liberty and corrupting the process through its favoritism and gifts to particular candidates. Led by Clay and Webster in the Senate, the National Republicans expressed appropriate indignation over Jackson's actions, and the president's related assumption of power. After acrimonious, almost violent debate, the Senate failed to override the veto, and Congress adjourned.

The opposition feigned outrage, but many were delighted at the outcome. Jackson had attacked a popular institution and laid out a set of controversial principles. In doing so, he had given the National Republicans arguably their greatest issue for the fall campaign. Jackson's assertion of executive power was novel and breathtaking. Not only did he claim to represent all the populace, but as head of a co-equal branch of government, he could also interpret the Constitution and challenge legislation that could threaten the freedom of Americans. To Jackson's thinking, no provision in the Constitution clearly gave exclusive power of interpretation to the Supreme Court. Moreover, Congress needed to consider the president's views as it constructed a legislative agenda. Ironically, Jackson's claims for the broadening of executive authority at the federal level might be seen as at odds with ancillary language in the veto message touting states' rights. The "true strength" of the government, he contended, "consists in leaving individuals and states as much as possible to themselves."

By destroying the BUS, Jackson sought to rectify Congress's mistaken overreach made in 1816—the establishment of a corporation that grew so large and abusive that it had to be brought down. How would the American people respond to such a bold move?[25]

Jacksonian Victory

As fall approached, the Democratic campaign swung into high gear. The Hickory Clubs organized torchlight parades through towns, with the faithful bearing portraits of the president, and held barbeques, infused with appropriate levels of whiskey, and where the campaign song, "The Hickory Tree," was enthusiastically sung:

> Hurra for the Hickory Tree!
> Hurra for the Hickory Tree!
> Its branches will wave o'er tyranny's grave
> And bloom for the brave and the free.

The Jacksonian print propaganda machine reached striking levels of effectiveness. Not only newspapers, but pamphlets, broadsides, song sheets, and cartoons circulated widely throughout the country, extolling the president's virtues and defense of American liberty against the onslaught of the advantaged. The most enduring cartoon from the campaign, however, emanated from the National Republicans, and depicted Jackson as "King Andrew" trampling upon the Constitution.

A justifiably concerned Jackson escalated electioneering by attending party events, shaking hands, and conversing with the masses. He did not engage in excessive campaigning, but if an event was held along his travel route, it was appropriate to stop and inspire his followers. The opposition ridiculed him for "descending in person into the political arena." They failed to see the new face of American democracy. The campaign became exciting and emotional. With such issues as the bank exploding to the surface, Democrats launched passionate attacks on the National Republicans as agents of wealth and privilege. In turn, the Clay forces lashed out at the president as a despot and military chieftain who had seized extraordinary power belonging to Congress and the people.

The masses disagreed, and awarded Jackson a decisive victory. His triumph in the electoral college was resounding (219 to 49), taking seventeen states to six for Clay. Disgruntled South Carolinians cast their ballots for Virginia Governor John Floyd, while Anti-Masonic nominee William Wirt captured Vermont. Jackson defeated Clay by the wide popular vote margin of 55 per cent to 37 percent, with the remainder scattered. Although this figure represented a slight decline in his percentage from 1828, Jackson's vote increased by over 40,000 from the previous election.

The Democratic political machine, effective for its time, made a difference in rallying the faithful and turning out the vote. Certainly, missteps had occurred and support lost or squandered over the Eaton Affair, the cabinet implosion, Calhoun's alienation, and squabbles over patronage. More importantly, Jackson himself put his presidency on the line by taking positions on contentious issues such as Indian removal, internal improvements, the BUS, and the tariff. Somehow Old Hickory had overcome both self-made problems and controversy over public policy. The National Republicans relentlessly derided Jackson's grab for power, crying out "tyranny" and "despotism," while the president offered Americans a simple choice regarding his actions and decisions. By November 1832, the voice of the people had been clearly heard, and Jackson was about to face a new round of challenges.[26]

Notes

1 Robert Remini, *Andrew Jackson and the Course of American Freedom 18-22-1832* (New York: Harper and Row, 1981), 144–55; Jon Meacham, *American Lion: Andrew Jackson in the White House* (New York: Random House, 2008), 4–6; H.W. Brands, *Andrew Jackson: His Life and Times* (New York: Anchor Books, 2006), 403–05.

2 Remini, *American Freedom*, 156–59; AJ to William Donelson, January 30, 1830, *Jackson Papers*, VIII, 60.
3 Remini, *American Freedom*, 173–80; Donald B. Cole, *The Presidency of Andrew Jackson* (Lawrence: University Press of Kansas, 1993), 32–34.
4 Ibid., 39–46; Remini, *American Freedom*, 167–69, 15–27; Jackson's First Inaugural Message, March 4, 1829, in James D. Richardson, ed., *A Compilation of the Messages and Papers of the Presidents*, II, (Washington, 1904), 436–38, Jackson's First Annual Message to Congress, December 8, 1829, ibid., 442–62.
5 Remini, *American Freedom*, 159–66; Mark R. Cheathem, *Andrew Jackson: Southerner* (Baton Rouge: Louisiana State University Press, 2013), 119–20; Cole, *Presidency of Jackson*, 26–32.
6 John Marszalek, *The Petticoat Affair: Manners, Mutiny, and Sex in Andrew Jackson's White House* (New York: Free Press, 1997), 22–44; Remini, *American Freedom*, 161–63; Cheathem, *Southerner*, 121–24.
7 Ibid., Marszalek, *Petticoat Affair*, 45–74, 139–46.
8 Ibid., 75–105; Remini, *American Freedom*, 205–10; Cheathem, *Southerner*, 123–28; Meacham, *American Lion*, 110–15.
9 Marszalek, *Petticoat Affair*, 157–79; Cheathem, *Southerner*, 124–26, Jon Meacham, *American Lion: Andrew Jackson in the White House* (New York: Random House, 2008), 145–54.
10 James Parton, *The Life of Andrew Jackson*, (New York: Mason Brothers, 1860), 287; Cole, *Presidency of Jackson*, 84–87.
11 Cheathem, *Southerner*, 125–26, 133–35; Remini, *American Freedom*, 234–36; Burstein, *Passions*, 188–92.
12 Remini, *American Freedom*, 240–47; Cole, *Presidency of Jackson*, 79–82.
13 Ibid., 63–66; Remini, *American Freedom*, 251–56.
14 Andrew K. Frank, "Native American Removal," in Adams, *Companion*, 391–402.
15 Ibid., 403–08; Remini, *American Freedom*, 257–65; Cheathem, *Southerner*, 153–58; Burstein, *Passions*, 184–88; Heidlers, *Indian Removal*, 25–28, 32–45; Cole, *Presidency of Jackson*, 68–74.
16 Ibid., 138–45.
17 Meacham, *American Lion*, 201.
18 Cole, *Presidency of Jackson*, 141.
19 Remini, *Election of Andrew Jackson*, 171–80; John Niven, *Martin Van Buren and the Romantic Age of American Politics* (New York: Oxford University Press, 1983), 196–99; Joel Silbey, *Martin Van Buren and the Emergence of American Popular Politics* (New York: Rowman and Littlefield, 2002), 52–53; Cole, *Presidency of Jackson*, 106–08; Remini, *American Freedom*, 358–60; Jackson to James Hamilton, Jr., June 29, 1828, *Jackson Papers*, VI, 476–77.
20 Robert Remini, *Andrew Jackson and the Bank War* (New York: Norton, 1967), 23–48; Cole, *Presidency of Jackson*, 96–99; Stephen Mihm, The Fog of War: Jackson, Biddle, and the Destruction of the Bank of the United States," in Sean P. Adams, ed. *A Companion to the Era of Andrew Jackson* (Malden, MA: Blackwell, 2013), 349–56.
21 Remini, *Bank War*, 51–64; Mihm, "Fog of War," 356–58.
22 Ibid., 361; Remini, *Bank War*, 73–80; Cheathem, *Southerner*, 160–63.
23 Remini, *American Freedom*, 364–66.
24 Ibid., 367–73; Cole, *Presidency of Jackson*, 100–06; Cheathem, *Southerner*, 162–64; Remini, *Bank War*, 51–56.
25 Cole, *Presidency of Jackson*, 102–06; Remini, *Bank War*, 70–78, 81–85; Mihm, "Fog of War," 359–61; Meacham, *American Lion*, 209–12; Remini, *American Freedom*, 364–73.
26 Meacham, *American Lion*, 218–20; Remini, *American Freedom*, 382–92; Remini, *Bank War*, 88–108; Cole, *Presidency of Jackson*, 148–52.

CHAPTER 5

THE WHITE HOUSE YEARS

SECOND TERM (1833–1837)

Jackson rushed to Nashville to escape the heat of a Washington summer, returning to the White House in late October, just in time to savor his triumph at the polls. Removed from the frenzy of the campaign's final weeks, the Hermitage restored his health and humor. On familiar ground, surveying crops and fields and entertaining family and friends gave him some sense of tranquility. Too often, that peace of mind was hard-earned. Jackson struggled to find a competent overseer, employing three during his presidency, and firing each of them for their perceived mismanagement of the slaves, cotton, and hogs. The Hermitage housed almost one hundred slaves, and Jackson's concern for them was both economic and personal. He expected obedience and productivity, and, in return, they deserved to be well treated and cared for. Ideally, Andrew Jr., his adopted son now in his early 20s, should have handled many of the responsibilities at the Hermitage. Jackson tried, but, sadly, his son's failures were many and ongoing. Some blame can be placed on the parents for coddling and not adequately preparing the young man for managing a plantation. Jackson tried to compensate by instructing him from afar on sales of crops and livestock, as well as on purchases and treatment of slaves. Andrew wrestled with financial matters, a problem not helped by his fondness for bourbon.

The situation became so serious by 1835 that Jackson, fearful for his son's behavior and the family's reputation, asked Andrew to abandon alcohol. He agreed. Perhaps Junior's handling of a devastating fire at the Hermitage in October 1834 was most revealing for Jackson. The blaze destroyed the roof and swept through the second floor of the building. Andrew Jr. was entrusted with supervising the reconstruction, which took almost two years and cost Jackson double the $2,500 he had budgeted for the repairs.

The general seemed particularly frustrated with Andrew's spending habits, regularly lecturing him on living more frugally and avoiding debt.

Nor was Andrew the smoothest young swain in Nashville, and several failed courtships prompted his father to try to find him the proper wife. No need. In November 1831, Junior soon met and married Sarah Yorke of Philadelphia. Interestingly, Old Hickory, immersed in working on his annual message in nearby Washington, failed to attend the wedding. Real joy soon came out of the marriage for Jackson in the presence of his first grandchild. Sarah gave birth to a girl on November 1, 1832. He had watched the pregnancy progress at the Hermitage, and urged Andrew Jr. to name the child Rachel. Less than two years later, Andrew III was also born. The proud grandfather delighted in both children, unapologetically admitting that "Little Rachel" was "as wild as a little partridge, & a little petted and spoiled," while little Andrew was "a fine stout fellow."[1]

The Nullification Crisis

Jackson had too little time to reflect on the joy of his burgeoning family. South Carolinians had spent the summer scuffling and grumbling over the new tariff; the discontent manifested itself in everything from irate editorials to bloody fistfights. For many Carolinians, the tariff represented more than an economic burden; it struck at the heart of the slavery issue. The major danger to the institution emanated from a consolidated federal government wielding its power through an expanded interpretation of the Constitution. To yield to Washington on the tariff would signal southern weakness, and perhaps pave the way for an aggressive assault on slavery. By 1831, William Lloyd Garrison and his provocative Boston newspaper, *The Liberator,* contributed to the growing outrage of abolitionists in the North. Assuring his readers that he would not compromise, Garrison promised, "I am in earnest—I will not equivocate—I will not excuse—I will not retreat an inch and I WILL BE HEARD." Meanwhile, slaves had shown their willingness to use violence. In August, bondsman Nat Turner initiated an uprising in southeastern Virginia that resulted in the murder of 60 whites and subsequent execution of 17 African Americans. Many others were beaten or deported. The threats were real. White Southerners believed that they must be resistant and resilient.[2]

South Carolina was not unified, however, in its antipathy towards a strong and perpetual nation. The state retained a solid number of Unionists, led by veteran diplomat and politician Joel Poinsett, who rejected the call by extremists to nullify the tariff. Those Unionists kept the president informed regarding evolving political and military activity. Retaining possession of the forts in Charleston harbor was particularly important, so Jackson ordered both the army and navy to be prepared for an emergency. While Jackson thought that calmer heads would ultimately prevail, he recognized that the federal government must be ready for the worst-case scenario.

Democratic Senator George M. Dallas of Pennsylvania looked on in amazement as events unfolded. "He is a much abler man than I thought him," Dallas remarked about Jackson in December 1832, "one of those naturally great minds which seem ordinary, except when the fitting emergency arises." Indeed, an emergency had arisen. In a swift-moving series of events in late November, a South Carolina convention nullified the Tariffs of 1828 and 1832. The assemblage also capped tariff rates at 12 percent, a number the Carolinians assumed was sufficient to provide the funds needed to operate the federal government. To back up their actions, Governor James Hamilton requested the legislature to approve a force of 12,000 men to defend Charleston against a potential federal invasion.[3]

Stunned by events in the state, a grim and resolute president responded to the threat with a clear statement of principle. "Our federal Union it must be preserved" had become more than Jefferson Day rhetoric. On December 10, Jackson the nationalist hurriedly penned a document of almost 9,000 words—the Nullification Proclamation—defending the Union. He contended that "we the People" constructed a nation and wrote the Constitution, forming "a *government,* not a league." The nullifiers argued that "we the states" had fashioned a compact and produced the Constitution, a notion Jackson rejected out of hand. For Old Hickory, the principle of the people ruling, not the states, was critical. Moreover, the states had surrendered elements of their sovereignty when they signed the Constitution and their residents became citizens of the United States. Admittedly, the states held onto certain prerogatives. As a life-long defender of states' rights, the president accepted the importance of states as a safeguard against possible violations of liberty and excesses by the federal government. The tenth amendment had granted all powers not specifically delegated in the Constitution to them. Jackson reaffirmed that idea, specifically in his opposition to federally funded internal improvements.

Yet matters defined by congressional law must take precedence. A rogue state employing its own policies for its own ends would invite chaos and disunion. Nullification was more than "contradicted expressly by the letter of the Constitution," Jackson claimed. Using words such as "incompatible," "inconsistent," "unauthorized," and "destructive" to describe the theory, he cautioned the people of South Carolina of the dire consequences "that must inevitably result from an observance of the dictates of the convention."

Jackson found secession equally distasteful and illegal. He called the concept a "revolutionary act" that could only be accomplished by "gross error" in interpreting the Constitution. "To say that any state may at pleasure secede from the Union is to say that the United States are not a nation." As for resistance to federal law, Jackson was clear in his challenge and the possible penalties. "Disunion by armed force is treason," he menaced, "are you really ready to incur its guilt?" Radicals might well be pushing this agenda, and, Jackson vowed, "on their heads be the dishonor, but on yours may fall the punishment."[4]

The president stood on solid ground, but he confronted a multi-faceted dilemma. The more obvious problem was deciding how to isolate the Palmetto State from its southern sisters. Clearly, sympathizers had raised their voices, especially Governor John Floyd of Virginia, a compatriot of Calhoun, who seriously considered military force if U.S. troops marched through his state. "I nor my country will be enslaved without a struggle," Floyd promised a correspondent. Similar protests could be heard throughout the South from Mississippi into North Carolina. Could Jackson and his supporters convince southerners who despised the tariff, but loved the Union that they needed to stand with the president and patiently support the modest reductions in the 1832 legislation?[5]

Critically, Jackson was dealing with the concurrent problem of negotiating Indian treaties and implementing the removal legislation passed by Congress in 1830. If he indicated weakness, hesitancy, or backpedaling on pushing the tribes beyond the Mississippi, those states desirous of Indian land might join with South Carolina for reasons beyond the tariff. When Georgia challenged the federal treaties with the Indians, the president's reluctance to support the Supreme Court and the Cherokee informs us about Jackson's priorities and his political awareness. Demonstrating an obvious inconsistency in the application of his philosophy, Old Hickory denied South Carolina the right to challenge a federal law, but was silent amidst the crisis with Georgia. Certainly, he endorsed removal and was unwilling to marshal a national military force to protect the Indians against the onslaught of the settlers. Whether such a strategy would have succeeded is highly uncertain, but his position was clear. In the case of South Carolina, Jackson not only denied the concepts of nullification and secession, but also defiantly asserted his intent to use the military to bring the radicals in line with the law.

Several anecdotes bring Jackson's lethal attitude into sharp focus. The general purportedly notified a South Carolina congressman that if violence erupted, "I will hang the first man of them I can get my hands on to the first tree I can find." He similarly told Van Buren that "Calhoun ought to be hung as a traitor." Senator Thomas Hart Benton of Missouri recalled a conversation with Senator Robert Y. Hayne of South Carolina where the Carolinian posed the question, "I don't really believe he would hang anybody, do you?" Benton recalled the general's summary execution of Arbuthnot and

Ambrister in Florida, and offered a direct and chilling reply, "I tell you, Hayne, when Jackson begins to talk about hanging, they can begin to look for the ropes."[6]

The language is revealing. Many Americans viewed their president as a man of both passion and action who was willing to defend the Union at all costs. Herein also rested a problem. Jackson assumed that he represented the people, and his two decisive electoral and popular victories confirmed that view. During the first term, his stance on issues, including several controversial vetoes, and his assertion of the White House as a co-equal branch of government deeply troubled his opponents. While some National Republicans applauded his unionism, others leveled charges of despotism. More than partisan rhetoric, they saw Congress as the voice of the people, with Jackson boldly usurping that power. His assumption of authority in the nullification crisis fueled those fears, prompting even some who supported him into a posture of cautious watching and waiting.

Old Hickory was not bluffing. If South Carolina fulfilled its pledge to flout the government and refused to collect, or allow the federal agents to collect, tariff duties commencing on February 1, 1833, Jackson would meet that challenge with military action. The president, with the assistance of Secretary of the Treasury Louis McLane, crafted a measure labeled the Force Bill. This ominous piece of legislation gave him an explicit mandate to react to the situation in South Carolina. He would be empowered to send the navy to Charleston to collect the customs duties at the U.S. forts in the harbor, and to use the American army and state militias to carry out federal laws. Calhoun, returned to the Senate, spoke fervently against the measure, defending the notion of secession, and denouncing the president's bullying and intimidation, "and for so doing it is that we are threatened to have our throats cut, and those of our wives and children." The rhetoric was perhaps extreme, but effective. A coalition of southern nullifiers and National Republicans recoiled at the notion of granting the president broad powers to bring the rebellious state to heel. Instead, Congress stalled the measure, with everyone searching for a more tranquil solution.[7]

Calhoun had support for his fundamental views, but by the end of January the other southern states decided not to confront the president and to stand by the Union. Jackson was also strengthened by the sympathy and, eventually, the backing of a number of National Republicans, including Clay and Webster. Fortunately for the president, Clay played a major role in helping to avert a possible civil war. In February, the Kentuckian brought his own conciliation bill and rate schedule to the Senate floor. He emerged as the element of reason between Calhoun and Jackson, "the Great Compromiser" offering to trade a lower tariff for the passage of the Force Bill. Congress responded, endorsing both measures by March 1. The revised duties gradually lowered the rates to 20 percent over the coming decade, and the next day Jackson signed the proposals into law. South Carolina agreed to repeal its nullification ordinance of the Tariffs of 1828 and 1832, but promptly and gratuitously nullified the offensive Force Bill.

The crisis had passed and compromise triumphed, at least momentarily, with everyone claiming victory. Clay received credit for his deal-making, and simultaneously appeared to take the edge off of Old Hickory's drive for executive power. The Calhounites got their reduced tariff rates and could pretend that they maintained the principle of nullification. The president, who had earlier recommended lower duties, had no real issue with the compromise, and he, too, could rejoice in the outcome. The Union had been preserved, and South Carolina had not carried through on its threats. Jackson demonstrated both leadership and resolve in facing down the radicals, but the estimation of his triumph proved overly optimistic. "Nullification is dead," he told a friend in May 1833. Perhaps this was true for his generation, but the seeds of disunion were only dormant, rising again in the 1840s as the Mexican-American War and slavery provided the genesis of the next crisis.[8]

The Bank War

While the outcome of the South Carolina crisis brought personal satisfaction, and even talk of a new Unionist party, Jackson offered no new expansive federal agenda in his second term. He realized, however, that unfinished business, including Indian removal and the controversy over the Bank of the United States was far from concluded. Jackson's veto and his subsequent election triumph proved to be only the first round in a struggle that lasted until the institution's charter expired in 1836. During those four years, Nicholas Biddle and the National Republicans continued to wage war with the president over the management of the Bank and the relocation of the government's deposits. This became a no-holds-barred brawl that dramatically affected the economy and brought censure to the White House.

Instability in the cabinet continued to be a problem. Jackson instead placed greater trust in the counsel of his old friends in the informal Kitchen Cabinet. The death of Tennesseans John Coffee and John Overton in 1833 deprived him of the advice of loyalists who had no personal political ambition. The cabinet that met on March 19, 1833 to commence the second administration appeared more competent than those who had served in 1829: Edward Livingston in the State Department, Louis McLane in the Treasury, Roger B. Taney as Attorney General, Lewis Cass in the War Department, Levy Woodbury in the Navy, and William Barry who continued as Postmaster General. Yet the rotation in the formal advisory body reached troubling new heights as his second term progressed; in total, four secretaries of state, five secretaries of the treasury, three attorney generals, three secretaries of war, three secretaries of the navy, and two postmasters general served over the eight years. Would this new cabinet be more loyal than the initial group that had resigned amidst the Eaton scandal?

The president continued to be concerned about the safety of the government's funds in the BUS, and Biddle's power to direct Bank monies into political campaigns that might undermine the Democrats. Would Biddle perhaps make another run at a re-charter measure? Jackson determined that the pressure must be kept on the BUS and the government's deposits removed as soon as possible. The president might in the future support a new national bank located in Washington and controlled by the federal government. For the present, however, he wanted the nation's funds placed in accounts in state banks. Since he had been broadly attacked for his heavy-handedness in the recent nullification crisis, Jackson attempted to build consensus by polling his cabinet on this removal and deposit issue. The result stunned him. Except for Attorney-General Taney, the entire cabinet supported the Bank and opposed the removal of the deposits. The Democratically controlled House of Representatives mirrored that view when it voted in early March 1833 by a two-to-one margin to retain the funds in the BUS accounts.[9]

Jackson was undeterred. A conservative fiscal policy for the country was another of his principles. He believed that paying the national debt, limiting expenditures for internal improvements, and ensuring the safety of the government's funds remained imperative. The Bank persisted as a danger and the sooner it died, the better off his administration and the American people would be. The president hoped that removing millions of dollars in government deposits would weaken public confidence in the BUS, harm its economic position, and ultimately accelerate its demise. Secretary of the Treasury McLane had expressed his well-reasoned objections to such a policy in measured language. The president appreciated McLane's candor, and wanted to keep him in the cabinet. Since he could not be counted upon to cooperate on the deposit issue, however, McLane was shifted to the State Department, and, in June 1833, Philadelphia banker William J. Duane assumed the Treasury post.

Jackson hastened the process by appointing trusted friend Amos Kendall to scout state banks that were both fiscally sound and loyal to the Democratic Party. By fall, Kendall presented a list of seven banks in Boston, New York, Philadelphia, and Baltimore that met the requirements. Jackson planned to act before Congress reconvened in December and could organize to thwart his policy. An added problem soon emerged when Duane refused to cooperate with the removal order. Whether prompted by pride or philosophy, Duane put the president in the uncomfortable situation of forcing the banker's dismissal after less than four months in office. The dependable Roger Taney, who helped draft Jackson's Bank veto message in July, moved over from Attorney General to Treasury on an interim basis to expedite matters. The grousing extended beyond Duane, however, and Old Hickory dreaded the embarrassment of another cabinet collapse. He labored hard, and successfully, to keep the disgruntled McLane and Cass in their positions.[10]

On October 1, 1833, Jackson moved to extend the power of the presidency to new heights. By Executive Order, the government's funds in the BUS were utilized to pay off existing federal obligations and debts. Any new monies accruing to the Treasury, usually through taxes, tariffs, or land sales, were placed in the seven "pet banks" identified by Kendall. Over time, the dollars in the BUS would be drained, and the relationship between Washington and the Monster Bank severed forever.

With the right team in place, the process moved without delay. By the end of the year, the government's deposits of almost $10 million were being withdrawn from the BUS and another fifteen new pet banks chosen as repositories. The solid foundation and fiscal responsibility of these banks, numbering over one hundred by the time Jackson departed the White House, proved to be uneven and certainly controversial. Many of the institutions had intimate ties to leading Democrats, hardly a foundation for fiscal responsibility. Ominously, the president had commenced this overhaul of the management of the nation's finances without consulting Congress.[11]

Nicholas Biddle realized that he was in a tightening vice. Within a week of Jackson's order, he swayed his board of directors into sharply restricting the Bank's loan policies. The scheme slowed the financial markets down to a crawl by limiting the credit and cash flowing into the economy. Without the influx of new money, businessmen struggled to expand their industries and farmers to buy more land. Biddle hoped their distress would reverberate in Washington and pressure the Congress into a renewed effort to charter the Bank.

His plan succeeded at two levels. First, the country was thrown into a recession, with rising bankruptcies and unemployment. The press widely reported the financial collapse and the ensuing misery of the populace. Many people recognized Biddle's role in manipulating the economy, but Jackson's stubborn behavior merited partial blame. Second, the Bank War of 1833–1834 crystallized opposition to the general. Separate groups (those who disagreed with Jackson on states' rights, Indian removal, internal improvements, the Bank, and tariff, including some dissident Democrats) could unify in their hatred of Old Hickory. They found common cause in his high-handed assumption of executive power, and soon began calling themselves "Whigs." The political party in England that had long opposed the monarch's exercise, or abuse, of authority lent their name to those in the United States who resisted the tyranny of "King Andrew I."[12]

The BUS was, after all, a congressionally chartered institution, and congressmen were furious at Jackson for removing the government's monies without their sanction. The vitriolic speeches ripping into the president, especially by Clay, Webster, and Calhoun, sometimes went on for days. The attacks reached a crescendo in February 1834, when the Senate not only rejected the nomination of Taney as Secretary of the Treasury, but, by a vote of 26 to 20, censured Jackson for his removal of the deposits. The act of censure did not reverse the policy, but embarrassed a man who placed great emphasis upon honor and reputation. Jackson responded at length in "The Protest," defending his actions, and, more importantly, reaffirming his view that he proceeded as he did because "the President is the direct representative of the American people." The Whigs were well aware of this most recent challenge to congressional power, and the Clay, Webster, Calhoun triumvirate responded again with blistering attacks on the Senate floor. The Kentuckian sounded the trumpet call to rise against despotism:

> We are in the midst of revolution, hitherto bloodless, but rapidly tending towards a total change of the pure republican character of government, and to the concentration of all power in the hands of one man . . . the government in eight years will have been transformed into an elective monarchy—the worst of all forms of government . . . and if Congress does not apply an instantaneous and effective remedy the fatal collapse will soon come on and we shall die— ignobly die, base, mean, and abject slaves.

The issue had now become a contest, inside and outside the capital, to win popular acceptance of which branch of government should be pre-eminent and most legitimately represented the masses. History has been on Jackson's side. While both scholars and the people debate the wisdom of an "imperial presidency," the power of the executive has dramatically increased over the past century and a half. The historian Remini dubbed Old Hickory the first modern president. He used his position for national leadership, and "strengthened the presidency, redefined its role, and profoundly altered its relationship to the American people." In January 1837, in a final moment of victory for Jackson, the Democratically controlled Senate expunged his censure by drawing large black lines in the printed record around the offensive resolution.[13]

Biddle's Bank expired with a whimper in 1836. The Pennsylvania legislature chartered the institution for five more years as a state bank, until it fell victim to financial damages inflicted by risky management and the ongoing depression. In 1844, Biddle died of bronchitis. The bank's demise left the country with no national currency until the Civil War. Ever vigilant about the rebirth of the monster, House Democrats crushed efforts to recharter the BUS by wide margins in April 1834, and Congress reaffirmed the pet banks as repositories for federal funds. The administration found it as difficult to develop a strategy to rein in the 22 new pet banks as it did to contain the old national bank and its 25 branches. Even with the problems, by 1836, the Treasury's deposits had been transferred from the BUS to the pet banks.

How then do we judge the practical outcome of Jackson's tightfisted economic policy, destroying the national bank, and moving towards a greater reliance on "pet banks? In the short term, the strategy seemed effective. In January 1835, Democrats toasted the accomplishment of the long sought-after objective of payment of the national debt. The country found itself in the unusual and enviable position of deciding what to do with the surplus revenues generated from taxes and tariffs. Congress, with bipartisan support, crafted a plan that might be fiscally dangerous, but would further stimulate the economy. In June 1836, it passed the Deposit Bill providing for the distribution of excess funds to the states, commencing in six months and in three annual installments. The measure also ensured that each state or territory would have one bank, and more than doubled the number of deposit sites that could receive these dollars from 33 to 81. But too much money loaned throughout the country by too many institutions with too few controls could have disastrous results.

Jackson had very real fears about the consequences. He seriously contemplated a veto of the bill, counted the votes in Congress, and then pulled back. His initial concerns proved accurate. Public land sales that might typically maximize annually at $5 million skyrocketed to $25 million in 1836. The additional dollars pumped into the economy often came from investors, sparking a wild speculation in government-owned western lands. In an effort to harness the boom, Jackson issued the Specie Circular in July, demanding that the public lands be paid for in gold and silver. The policy worked, and land sales were sharply curtailed.

However, the country fell into a serious depression, the Panic of 1837, the following year. The extent to which the absence of the BUS and Jackson's hard money policies contributed to the economic collapse is controversial. Arguably, the existence of a national bank with its central currency and controls may well have assisted the nation in recovering from a downturn that lasted until 1843. Whether the BUS could have prevented a depression is another matter.

Suprisingly, prominent scholars agree in their broader evaluation of the Bank controversy. Robert Remini, Old Hickory's sympathetic biographer, concedes that the BUS was a worthy establishment that benefited the U.S. and the American people. Unfortunately, it became "caught in a death struggle between two willful, proud, stubborn men" and beyond the point of agreement. Whig historian Daniel Walker Howe contends that the general's ultimate triumph brought few tangible benefits to the masses. Compromise and government supervision should, however, have saved the BUS. "Jackson and Biddle were both too headstrong for the country's good," Howe posits. "The great Bank War turned out to be a conflict both sides lost." Jon Meacham writes the epitaph for the institution: "The Bank was neither as venal as the Jacksonians argued nor as indispensable as Biddle's friends asserted."

As for the panic, the complex root cause involved not only the government's policies, but those of the global marketplace. London bankers and investors cut back loans and demanded specie as payment for debts, revealing that events taking place in Great Britain and China could impact production, demand, and prices at a Massachusetts mill or on a Mississippi plantation. The United States received a rather primitive and painful welcome to the global economy well before the twentieth century.[14]

Assaults on the President

Not surprisingly, Andrew Jackson was a literal and figurative target for his enemies. Of the presidents in office during the early republic, perhaps only Thomas Jefferson generated such hostile public and private feelings among his contemporaries. The Virginian's opponents saw dangers equally in the ideas and philosophy of the man, as in the man himself. Federalists attacked Jefferson as an atheist, a disbeliever who would close churches. They claimed he championed the mob whose involvement in government would ruin the vision of the Founding Fathers. His limited interpretation of the Constitution and narrow states' rights views would likewise cripple the unity and economic future of the country. Moreover, as a dedicated Francophile, he would deliver the nation's destiny not only into the hands of the Devil, but also to, the French. Beyond the political, the personal attacks included broadsides and ballads revealing Jefferson's hypocritical fathering of several children with Sally Hemings, a young slave at Monticello.

Jackson was the object of similar slings and arrows. The attacks on his marriage and relationship with Rachel accelerated until her untimely death in 1828. The accompanying reminders of his violent temper, duels, and military aspirations, harkening back to his occupation of New Orleans in 1815, never disappeared. Clay reminded the Senate of these dangers in his aforementioned speech in February 1834; the Old Hero aroused very real anxiety over his intentions to become a new Caesar. Numerous presidential actions had reinforced that viewpoint for his enemies, the scornful rhetoric sometimes accompanied by dramatic negative images and cartoons circulating among the public. And while most Americans perceived Jackson's frontier roots, unsophisticated writing style, and absence of intellectual pretension as qualities that put him in touch with the common folk, opponents delighted in mocking those same traits.

The president battled through recurring and serious health problems in June 1833, as he launched an exhausting tour of the Northeast. The public gatherings were large, riotous, and reassuring, and the private events filled with toasts, handshakes, and smiles. Approaching Baltimore, Jackson rode twelve miles on the new Baltimore and Ohio Railroad—the first chief executive to ride on a train. From Philadelphia to New York, the crowds confirmed the affection for him that they had expressed in the recent November election. As Jackson approached Boston, however, his travels took a more controversial turn. Harvard President Josiah Quincy had been vacillating over whether to award the president an honorary doctor of laws degree. Quincy finally decided that, in spite of the lack of formal education, Jackson's experience as a lawyer and judge qualified him for the award. The college event itself went well, with Old Hickory charming the skeptics at the ceremony and reception. John Q. Adams remained an exception. He refused an invitation, informing Quincy, "I could not be present to see my darling Harvard disgrace herself by conferring a Doctor's degree upon a barbarian and savage who could scarcely spell his own name."[15]

While insults and verbal attacks had become an essential component of the American political climate, physical assaults had no such place—at least until Jackson. The first such incident, occurring just prior to his Northeast tour, had its background in the controversial naval service of Virginian Robert B. Randolph. Lieutenant Randolph had served with valor in the War of 1812, and attained the rank of acting purser of the *U.S.S. Constitution* when Margaret Eaton's husband, John Timberlake, allegedly committed suicide in 1828. A Treasury Department audit in 1830, led by Kitchen Cabinet members Isaac Hill and Amos Kendall, revealed that $9,000 was missing from the ship's accounts. Randolph blamed Timberlake and reinforced the rumors that improper management of funds had probably affected Timberlake's decision. In a somewhat complicated and politically charged Senate investigation, which utilized the Treasury's audit, Timberlake was exonerated of any misdeeds and the blame for the absent monies fell on Randolph. The irate Virginian demanded a Naval Court of Inquiry, which muddled through the confusing evidence and testimony before agreeing in January 1833 that Randolph had unintentionally defrauded the government of more than $4,000. The Board, however, was uncertain whether or how to punish the officer and passed the duty along to the president.

Jackson reviewed the case and found that Randolph did, in fact, intend to defraud. On April 18, he directed the Secretary of the Navy to dismiss him from the service.

The discharge not only ended Randolph's career in the navy, but also seriously tarnished the standing of a proud and prominent Virginia family. Randolph, who claimed the government owed him $9,000 from his service on board the *Constitution*, reacted bitterly to the decision. The General Assembly in Virginia had recently presented him with a sword of honor for his gallant conduct in the War of 1812, and he believed that the Naval Board had exonerated him from any wrongdoing. Randolph fired off letters to newspapers blasting Jackson and threatening a law suit and an appeal to Congress. "If there be not honesty and firmness enough in the officers of the Treasury Department, to investigate the state of this concern," he wrote, "I will take it upon myself to bring it to an issue." With his honor and reputation in ruins, Randolph acted to avenge himself in the classic fashion of a southern gentleman.[16]

On May 6, 1833, the former lieutenant joined a festive throng, eager to meet the Old Hero aboard the Potomac River steamer, the *Sydney*, docked at Alexandria, Virginia. Jackson had just returned from a visit to Fredericksburg where he witnessed the unveiling of a monument to George Washington's mother, Mary. In spite of the reoccurring pain under his ribs, the president decided to greet the public. His discomfort prompted him to do so behind a table in his cabin, where he sat with a pipe clenched firmly between his teeth, clutching a newspaper, and greeting a steady stream of callers. Jackson had never met Randolph, and when the young man approached, the general simply apologized for not rising and extended his hand. Randolph reacted by grasping Jackson's nose, and turning it until blood flowed. Tweaking was the consummate insult to a southern male, as Jackson well knew. In typical fashion, he seized his cane and attempted to pursue Randolph out the door. Cabinet members and aides, including Andrew Jackson Donelson, intervened to prevent further damage, but in the ensuing chaos, the assailant escaped to a waiting horse, and out of the District of Columbia. Though a grand jury and a magistrate in the District of Columbia issued warrants for his arrest, Randolph found sanctuary beyond District laws in Virginia, a state governed by Calhoun supporter John Floyd, who was still smarting from the nullification crisis.[17]

Randolph received the backing of a number of newspaper editors for defending himself and his honor in the only possible way "against an indignant and cruel injustice" heaped upon him by the president. Many Virginians agreed. Society welcomed him with dinners and parties, and toasts were drunk in his honor. The administration remained in hot pursuit, however, and a federal marshal finally caught up with Randolph in Richmond.

He was arrested and imprisoned in November 1833 for violating a congressional law of 1820 regarding his improprieties with the funds aboard the *Constitution*. Outrage quickly followed, and rumors flew that Governor Floyd would use the state cavalry to prevent Randolph's extradition to the District of Columbia and that a mob was forming to free him from jail. Many Commonwealth residents seemed to share the view that Randolph was being indicted because of his assault on the president, not because of his financial misdeeds.

The two-week trial that began in December 1833 fell under the jurisdiction of Chief Justice John Marshall. In the case of the assault, Marshall, a nationalist who was stung by Jackson's contradictory positions to the Court on the Bank of the United States and Cherokee removal, supported the limited reach of government. He and federal District Judge Philip Barbour, who had earlier refused to grant an extradition order on jurisdictional grounds, claimed District law did not apply in Virginia. Now, Marshall, perhaps not surprisingly, found that the congressional law did not apply to Randolph since he was an *acting* purser. The charges against him were accordingly dismissed; he paid neither financial penalty to the government nor was he sentenced for his attack on the Old Hero.[18]

Less than two years later, following a series of death threats, Jackson survived a much more serious assault. On January 30, 1835, he emerged from the House chamber, having attended a funeral service for a South Carolina congressman. Accompanied by two cabinet members, Jackson was within ten feet of a "handsome, well dressed" young man who proceeded to draw a pistol and fire at the president. The cap exploded with a loud bang, but since the powder failed to ignite, the gun misfired. While Jackson, with his cane raised, rushed the attacker, a second pistol was fired and similarly failed. Somehow the president had escaped a probable death. The odds of both pistols not discharging were put at 125,000 to 1.

While many promptly determined that Jackson's life had been saved by Divine Providence who intended him to finish his term, science indicates that the misty air of a cool winter morning dampened the powder. Both pistols were later fired accurately and effectively at 30 feet. The individual charged with the offense, Richard Lawrence, was an unemployed English house painter. He claimed that Jackson had used his influence to keep him from his rightful place on the British throne. A jury justifiably found Lawrence insane and committed him to a Washington asylum for the remainder of his life. The president saw a deeper conspiracy, led by Mississippi Senator George Poindexter, to seek revenge after the recent tussles over nullification and the Bank. An investigation revealed no link between Lawrence and Poindexter, but Jackson remained unconvinced. His enemies, he felt, were relentless, and had now turned violent.[19]

The outcomes of the Randolph and Lawrence incidents merit attention at several levels. First, no previous chief executive had been assaulted, nor had the notion been contemplated by the Founding Fathers. Randolph had committed a crime in the federal District of Columbia, but no congressional law existed singling out the president for protection on a national scope. Since extradition was not forthcoming from Virginia, Randolph escaped punishment. Lawrence fired at Jackson in the Capitol, therefore he could be speedily tried and sentenced in Washington. Amazingly, Congress waited until 1965, following the death of John F. Kennedy, before passing legislation making the kidnapping or assassination of a president a federal crime.

Second, Jackson refused to allow the episodes to change the level of protection around the office. No Secret Service existed, and in a democracy, Old Hickory contended, there should be no military guard. Indeed, no security was present at the doors to the White House. Apparently, the president should be prepared at all times to defend himself from physical attack. Jackson already carried a sword cane, but had neither the time nor ability to deploy it effectively with either Randolph or Lawrence.

Third, Instead of being shocked and incensed at the attacks on Old Hickory, some Whig editors and politicians contended that these were personal assaults. The fact that the man in question happened to be president was only incidental.

While many were horrified at the news of the confrontations, the violence confirmed an Old World model in the thought of Jackson's opponents. From the days of ancient Rome, emperors and kings were the objects of assassination, not democratically elected presidents. The *Niles' Register* remarked that should such incidents occur in England they would be considered high treason, "but there is no king in the U.S.! We have no life guards to protect the persons of our Presidents nor government priests to direct their conscience . . . the person of the President is not more sacred than that of a representative of the people." If Old Hickory became a target, he had likely encouraged the incidents by his imperial behavior.

Finally, both attacks confirmed in Jackson's mind that, in their frustration, his enemies conspired to humiliate and even kill him. Failing to triumph on the issues, they resorted to dishonor and death to embarrass and finally remove him as man and president. Jackson was wrong about the conspiracies, and federal investigations failed to turn up any evidence in either case. Even so, Jackson convinced many Americans that these were attacks not just upon him, but on the institution of the chief executive, because he had fought to defend the Union and the people against forces seeking to subvert the nation and liberty.[20]

Foreign Affairs

Andrew Jackson's principles of good government included the process of top-down decision making. As reluctant cabinet members soon discovered, the Old Hero viewed policy as something to be created in consultation with, not determined by, his advisors. Jackson not only had strong concerns about domestic affairs, such as the BUS, Indian matters, tariffs, and internal improvements, but also in regard to foreign policy. Since he confronted so many critical domestic issues during his presidency, his contributions in advancing the place of the United States on the world stage are often marginalized. Jackson, the nationalist, advocated both commercial and territorial expansion. He embraced the notion of "Manifest Destiny" before the term was coined in the 1840s. The nation had a God-given right to control North America. Therefore, he had pushed for the seizure of Florida and Indian removal. Later, he desired the annexation of Texas, California, and all of the Oregon country. There was also a sense of mission. As he told the Congress in his first annual message, "Our great desire is to see our brethren of the human race secured in the blessings enjoyed by ourselves, and in the knowledge, in freedom and in social happiness." The increased American world presence came with accompanying risks. Jackson demanded that the United States be accorded the respect of the major powers; no small task given the size of the military in the 1830s.

Unfortunately, the president's own failings, as well as those of his advisors, hampered the attainment of his goals. In many ways, Jackson was parochial; he had never traveled outside the country, spoke no foreign language, and held a prejudice against Spanish-speaking nations. The general approached the State Department as he would an army, and had a tendency to micromanage as many aspects as possible, down to consular level appointments in remote cities. Predictably, rotation occurred too frequently. Four secretaries of state—Martin Van Buren, Edward Livingston, Louis McLane, and John Forsyth—occupied the office, with the Georgian Forsyth (1834–1837) serving the longest stint. Although talented men, none was allowed much freedom of movement. They endured for various lengths of time, promoting meaningful internal reform in the State Department, but only marginally affecting the course of action on the world stage. The president had his own agenda.

By 1830, the Jeffersonian vision of a small independent farmer tilling the soil with his wife and children, eking out a subsistence living, and bartering with local merchants had yielded to a larger dream. The market revolution following the War of 1812 encouraged Americans to grow surplus grains and cotton for sale in the U.S. and abroad. Similarly, emerging Northeastern factories produced textiles, shoes, and clocks for consumers worldwide.

The transition from subsistence agrarian to aspiring capitalist came with significant risks for many farmers. They borrowed money to purchase land, animals, and tools in the hope that the markets for their goods, and the accompanying profits, would remain strong. Their lifestyle could improve dramatically, unless, of course, prices plummeted, as they had in the Panic of 1819 and would again in 1837 and 1857. In that case, they could lose everything.

Jackson recognized this increased impetus for material success. Through hard work, smart decisions, and a fortunate marriage, he had risen from common roots to become an affluent planter. As president, he made the advancement of American commerce a major thrust of his foreign policy. He sought to expand the old markets of Europe and negotiate treaties in the newer markets of Asia, Latin America, and the Middle East. As a result, his agents secured commercial pacts with Great Britain, Russia, and Turkey. While the U.S. had engaged in limited trade with Asia and the Middle East since the 1780s, no commercial agreements had been signed. American merchants and ship owners still profited mightily from trading pepper from Sumatra, coffee from Mocha on the Red Sea, opiates from the Ottoman Empire, and tea from China. The Quallah Battoo incident and Edmund Roberts' mission provide two examples of Jackson's efforts to both defend and expand commerce in Asia.

On February 7, 1831, the *Friendship*, a pepper trader out of Salem, Massachusetts, was boarded by Sumatrans at the port of Quallah Battoo in the Indian Ocean. The natives overran the ship, killed several crew members, and removed the cargo of gold and opium. They left the pepper behind. Protests to the Sultan by the American commercial agent in the region yielded no satisfaction, and howls of concern, especially from New England ship owners and merchants, arose when the news reached U.S. shores months later. An angry Jackson moved aggressively, dispatching the thirty-six-gun frigate *Potomac* under the command of Captain John Downes to seek "restitution, indemnity, and the immediate punishment of the offenders." Downes was ordered to apprehend the persons responsible and inform the local rulers that a larger fleet would mete out "more ample punishment" if the attacks did not cease. In February 1832, the *Potomac* arrived off Quallah Battoo, a town of some 4,000 people, fully a year after the incident. The captain briefly considered negotiations before ordering the landing of some 250 marines in the middle of the night. The town fell after bloody fighting that resulted in two Americans killed and seven wounded. The Sumatrans lost at least 100 dead and perhaps more wounded. While Quallah Battoo was plundered and burned, a search found no cargo from the *Friendship* and no officials to interrogate. The mission had thus far achieved nothing but revenge. Downes evacuated the town and tried a different tactic. He bombarded it the next day until the white flag of surrender was raised. Enough damage had been done, and the emissaries of the rajah along the coast pledged their friendship to the United States.[21]

While the mission accomplished its desired effect in Asia, the National Republicans sought to use the incident for political advantage. The news broke in the press on July 10, the same day as the Bank veto. Opposition papers rushed to praise the gallant Captain Downes, while condemning the president for yet another shameful abuse of power. This time his actions were not only brash, but both unconstitutional and murderous. The Democrats characterized the natives as a band of unruly, uncivilized pirates. The opposition *Washington National Intelligencer* defended the "poor Malays" as a civilized people with government and the arts, whose women and children were brutally killed under Jackson's orders. With each retelling in the National Republican press, the number of casualties mounted. As the story became a national incident, Congress and the president were forced to act. The House of Representatives, controlled by the Democrats, launched an investigation that revealed Downes had indeed exceeded his orders. Jackson had stated that the captain should negotiate first, and if that failed, then attack. Downes attacked, then negotiated.

The National Republicans had hoped for the exposure of incriminating documents that would embarrass Jackson and open him to charges of abuse of power and the slaughter of innocents. The discredited captain was put on waiting orders at the Boston navy yard for three years and the political opposition retreated—losing their best foreign policy issue for the 1832 campaign. Old Hickory had demonstrated that he would take executive action and not tolerate attacks on American commerce anywhere in the world.

Most Americans agreed. The self-satisfied Democratic *Washington Globe* fired a campaign salvo in late July. "All that remains for us this summer is to guard against Mr. Clay and the cholera—the preventative to the first is to be found in the intelligence, purity and independence of the people—the remedy against the second is their cleanliness, temperance, and care. Let us look to these matters."[22]

On the heels of the Quallah Battoo incident, the president recognized that formal commercial relations with the Far East would both reduce the likelihood of further conflict and enhance the prospects of profits for American merchants and shippers. Secretary of the Navy Levi Woodbury of New Hampshire knew just the right man for the assignment—veteran New England sea captain Edmund Roberts. Roberts departed the U.S. in March 1832 bound for Muscat on the Red Sea, Sumatra, Cochin China (Vietnam), Siam (Thailand), and Japan. The Americans suspected that the rival British would attempt to subvert the mission, so Roberts travelled under the guise of the secretary to the captain of a navy sloop, the *U.S.S. Peacock*.

Roberts found the task daunting. He arrived in Sumatra after the *Potomac* had bombarded Quallah Battoo. Predictably, the local rajahs were in no mood to make concessions to the Americans, and a second visit some months later confirmed the hostile environment. Roberts made no effort to negotiate with the King of Acheen, the nominal ruler, and a man he branded a "powerless savage." Similar failure awaited him in Vietnam, where few had ever heard of the United States. The emperor finally agreed to see the emissary, if he agreed to "kowtow" (bow) before him and deliver his greeting from the president "in silent awe" and "with uplifted hands." A furious Roberts, who viewed the Vietnamese as an oppressed and semi-barbarous people, refused to humiliate himself or his nation. Sailing off to neighboring Siam, he spent two months negotiating with the king's representatives in Bangkok, and ultimately produced a commercial treaty. A second agreement was added in September 1833 when he signed a pact with his old friend, Sultan Seyed Syeed of Muscat.

Two years after his departure, in April 1834, Roberts arrived in Boston. He had failed in Sumatra and Vietnam, but succeeded in Siam and Muscat. Japan, an important goal, had been ignored because Roberts felt unprepared, especially in terms of appropriate gifts for the emperor. Encouraged by his modest accomplishments, the administration endorsed a second, better financed mission which followed in April 1835. The captain was instructed to revisit Vietnam and negotiate with Japan. Tragically, Roberts contracted cholera, limiting any talks in Vietnam, and prompting a visit to Canton, China where he died in June 1836. A decade before the mission of Caleb Cushing formally concluded a treaty with China, and two decades before Matthew Perry forced Japan to open its ports, the Jackson administration acted to explore and develop trade in the Orient. These pioneering efforts ushered in a century of increased American interest in the region.[23]

The Jacksonian vision of trade with the Far East, as well as with the west coast of North and South America, would be further enhanced by a passage linking the Atlantic and Pacific Oceans. The administration negotiated trade agreements with Mexico, Peru-Bolivia, Chile, and Venezuela that would be aided by the ability to move goods by road, railroad, or canal traversing Panama or Nicaragua. Consequently, in the fall of 1835, Jackson dispatched Charles Biddle, ironically a Democrat and the younger brother of BUS president Nicholas, to Central America. Biddle struggled with his role. Neglecting the instructions to visit Nicaragua, Biddle focused on Panama, where he became caught up in the politics and protocols of the parent nation, New Granada (Colombia). The Colombian government finally approved an agreement for steamship transit on the Chagres River and the building of a road, but the diplomat foolishly confused his public and private mission. Although employed by the State Department to advance American commerce and security, Biddle secured a contract that provided hundreds of thousands of acres of land and construction privileges for his firm, the Atlantic and Pacific Transportation Company.

Biddle returned triumphant to the U.S. in September 1836, but an angry Jackson deliberately refused to present his agreement to the Congress. The president added in his annual message of January 1837 that it was "not expedient" to open talks on the subject of a canal or railroad in Central America. Biddle's untimely death in December 1836 and the Panic of 1837 doomed any efforts of the company to proceed with the plan.

The Mexican War, the annexation of California, and the subsequent gold rush all confirmed the need for a trans-isthmian route. The British posed a real threat to American growth in the region, so the U.S. eventually negotiated the Clayton-Bulwer Treaty of 1850 to provide for mutual development in Central America and avoid conflict over canal construction. Washington also achieved accord with the Latin Americans for road and canal rights. By the 1850s, wealthy American businessmen Cornelius Vanderbilt and Charles Morgan battled each other for control of the transit routes. The Biddle mission, though unsuccessful, reflected the importance of the coastal trade in North and South America, and in the Far East, as well as the need to assist the oil-producing whaling fleets in the Pacific. The Roberts and Biddle missions generated bi-partisan support from Congress and the business community, and provided a rationale for expanding the navy.[24]

Jackson's plan was to broaden American commerce in the future while demanding respect for that commerce in the past. During the course of the Napoleonic Wars (1792–1815), Europeans subjected neutral U.S. shipping to a series of abuses, including the seizure of vessels, cargoes, and crew. Jacksonian diplomats persuaded Spain, Naples, Portugal, and Denmark to pay millions of dollars in damages, referred to as spoliations, to American merchants for their losses.

France remained reluctant. On July 4, 1831, Minister William Rives finally reached an agreement with French officials for $4.5 million in indemnities. Americans rejoiced, but unfortunately, the French Chamber of Deputies thought the amount too generous and refused to appropriate the funds. When, in the spring of 1834, the Chamber formally rejected the treaty, Jackson labeled the vote "unexpected and mortifying." Observing his reaction, Navy Secretary Levi Woodbury remarked he had never seen the president demonstrate "a more firm resolve to vindicate our rights and honor."[25]

Advisors bombarded Jackson with counsel regarding a possible response. Moderation prevailed in the short term, but by that winter it became apparent the French had no intention of fulfilling the obligation. Old Hickory, revealing another of his prejudices acquired from his time in New Orleans, informed his cabinet, "I know them French. They won't pay unless they're made to." Jackson became increasingly adamant. In his December 1834 annual message, he requested the power from Congress to launch reprisals by confiscating French ships and property in the U.S.—that is, if the Chamber did not appropriate the money owed at their next session. The Whig-controlled Senate refused to yield that authority to the president, and a storm of protest, led by Clay and Webster, arose once again accusing Jackson of seeking dictatorial powers. A fortifications bill passed the House, providing the executive with $3 million to strengthen the nation's defenses in the event of war. It met with hostility in the Senate.[26]

While Jackson failed to get the power he desired from Congress, his attitude and intent was clearly heard across the Atlantic. The French Chamber swiftly passed an appropriations bill in April 1835, but an amendment demanded that Jackson explain his threatening remarks in the December message. The president predictably saw such language as an inappropriate intrusion by the French into a communication between two branches of the American government. He would not be humiliated, disgraced, or explain or be forced to apologize.

Sabers rattled on both sides of the ocean. Jackson's confidants urged an even-tempered approach, and he wisely softened his language in his December 1835 message to Congress. While he would never stain the honor of his country by apologizing, the president declared, "The conception that it was my intention to menace or insult the Government of France is . . . unfounded." The French eagerly accepted the olive branch as sufficient to assuage their honor. By May 10, 1836, Jackson could inform the nation that the spoliation claims had been paid in full.[27]

As he exited the White House, the Old Hero rightfully declared that American claimants had received over $7 million: payments that other administrations sought but had been unable to secure. At the same time, the determination and assertiveness of the administration changed attitudes in Europe. No longer weak and compliant, the Americans demonstrated a forceful posture that commanded recognition. While far from the equal of the Old World in military might, the United States revealed a willingness to flex its muscle and demand respect. Concurrently, the president had shown that, while not a man to be trifled with, he could also be flexible and patient. The United States and its brash leader were emerging as a troublesome presence on the global stage.

Jackson had long believed that the national boundaries needed to be expanded. For purposes of agricultural growth and border security, Texas should be added to the Union. Both Jackson and John Quincy Adams had initially been hesitant to incorporate Texas, but political circumstances in

Mexico and U.S. ambitions changed their views on the subject. An unstable, independent Mexico included lands stretching from Texas to California that might be used more productively under American control. Hence Adams had proposed the purchase of Texas for $1 million during his presidency, and in 1829, Jackson increased the amount to $5 million. The Mexicans refused the offers. The following year, diplomat Anthony Butler was able, however, to obtain a favorable commercial treaty and finally settle the border between Texas and Louisiana at the Sabine River.

In the 1820s, the Mexicans had attempted to boost the population and development in their lightly settled northern province by inviting thousands of Americans, many southerners with slaves, into Texas. The rumblings of discontent with the rule of the Catholic, dark-skinned, Spanish-speaking Mexicans rapidly emerged. Talk of revolution, led by Jackson's old lieutenant, Sam Houston, jeopardized the purchase. If an uprising did occur, the U.S. government would be blamed for aiding and abetting the cause. Jackson much preferred to buy the territory from Mexico, much like Jefferson had obtained Louisiana from France, rather than raise anti-slavery hackles by prolonged debate over annexing a slave-owning independent country.[28]

If Jackson suspected the integrity of the French, he thought even less of the Spanish. When the subject of greed and Mexican public officials arose, Jackson displayed a deeper prejudice, remarking to Butler, "I scarcely ever knew a Spaniard who was not the slave of avarice." The president did, however, draw a line at bribing officials. Jackson rationalized that he could not control funds delivered to officials which might be used for private purposes. In contrast, it would be unacceptable to pay politicians directly with the expectation that they would vote for such a measure as the cession of Texas. Butler bypassed such considerations, reminding Jackson of the absence of character and the corruption in Mexican culture.

Regrettably for the Americans, the chaotic Mexican government could not be persuaded or bribed. Jackson fueled the fire in 1835 when he instructed Butler to offer an additional $500,000 for San Francisco Bay. The proposals for Texas and California imploded amidst the Revolution of 1835. The Texans won their independence within the year, and Jackson's fears of the difficulty of annexing the Lone Star Republic proved accurate. The United States, along with various European nations, recognized the newly independent country, but the deeply divisive slavery issue prohibited annexation until 1845.[29]

Jacksonian policy towards Mexico was a disaster. The president's poor choice of the inept and arrogant Butler contributed to the collapse of relations in the period. Jackson himself bears some responsibility. By assuming an abrasive attitude towards Mexico, he fostered a climate of distrust, even hostility, which helped pave the road towards the Mexican-American War of 1846.

When Old Hickory departed the presidency, he could take credit for a bold, assertive foreign policy that yielded mixed results. The triumphs in negotiating new European commercial arrangements and collecting the spoliations claims were not matched by similar successes with Mexico or in Central America. Efforts in Asia revealed a pioneering energy to expand trade and assure that American ships and cargoes would be protected by a watchful U.S. navy. Merchants waxed enthusiastically about the new trade possibilities with the British West Indies and Turkey, although commerce in the Far East and South America failed to meet the anticipated levels. Jackson simultaneously surprised and infuriated the Whigs with his direction and control of diplomacy, and his assumption and extension of executive authority.

Old Hickory's eight turbulent years in the White House had witnessed dramatic domestic developments as well. The tragic and controversial Indian removal, the crisis over the tariff and nullification, a divisive Bank war, and the struggle over internal improvements had splintered the Democratic Party, and given rise to a more purposeful Whig party passionately united in its hatred of Andrew Jackson. More troublesome, the animosity reached a level where the opposition found a way to defend those men who would assault the president.

Notes

1 Mark R. Cheathem, *Andrew Jackson: Southerner* (Baton Rouge: Louisiana State University Press, 2013), 142–51.
2 Ibid., 136–37; James Brewer Stewart, *William Lloyd Garrison and the Challenge of Emancipation* (Arlington Heights, IL: Harlan Davidson, 1992), 50–51.
3 Cheathem, *Southerner*, 137–38; Richard Ellis, *The Union at Risk: Jacksonian Democracy, States' Rights and the Nullification Crisis* (New York: Oxford University Press, 1987), 73–78; Robert Remini, *Andrew Jackson and the Course of American Freedom 18-22-1832* (New York: Harper and Row, 1981), 380–82.
4 Jon Meacham, *American Lion: Andrew Jackson in the White House* (New York: Random House, 2008), 222–35; Ellis, *Union at Risk*, 78–88; Andrew Jackson, Nullification Proclamation, December 10, 1832, Richardson, ed., *A Compilation of the Messages and Papers of the Presidents* (Washington: Government Printing Office, 1904) II, 640–56.
5 Meacham, *American Lion*, 232–34.
6 Ellis, *Union at Risk*, 75–78.
7 Meacham, *American Lion*, 238–41; Ellis, *Union at Risk*, 94–95.
8 Cheathem, *Southerner*, 139–41; Ellis, *Union at Risk*, 170–77.
9 Robert Remini, *Andrew Jackson and the Bank War* (New York: Harper and Row, 1977), 111–13; Sean Wilentz, *The Rise of American Democracy: From Jefferson to Lincoln* (New York: W.W. Norton, 2005), 392–93.
10 Ibid., 394–97; Robert Remini, *Andrew Jackson and the Bank War* (New York: W.W. Norton, 1967), 114–24.
11 Ibid., 125–26.

12 Ibid., 127–30; Sean Wilentz, *The Rise of Democracy: From Jefferson to Lincoln* (New York: WW Norton, 2005), 398–402.
13 Ibid., 398–400; Remini, *Jackson and the Bank War,* 135–48; John M. Belohlavek, "*Let the Eagle Soar!*": *The Foreign Policy of Andrew Jackson* (Lincoln: University of Nebraska Press, 1985), 37.
14 Donald B. Cole, *The Presidency of Andrew Jackson* (Lawrence: University Press of Kansas, 1993), 229–35; Remini, *Jackson and the Bank War,* 174–76; Daniel Walker Howe, *What Hath God Wrought: The Transformation of America, 1815–1848* (New York: Oxford University Press, 2007), 394–95; Meacham, *American Lion,* 212.
15 H.W. Brands, *Andrew Jackson: His Life and Times* (New York: Anchor Books, 2006), 485–86; Meacham, *American Lion,* 260–63.
16 John M. Belohlavek, "Assault on the President: The Jackson–Randolph Affair of 1833," *Presidential Studies Quarterly,* XII, Summer 1982, 362–63; Meacham, *American Lion,* 254–55.
17 Belohlavek, "Assault on the President," 361–62.
18 Ibid., 364–66.
19 Meacham, *American Lion,* 298–301; Cole, *Presidency of Jackson,* 221.
20 *Niles' Register,* June 8, June 22, 1833.
21 Belohlavek, *Let the Eagle Soar,* 152–56.
22 Ibid., 157–62; David F. Long, "Martial Thunder: The First Official American Armed Intervention in Asia," *Pacific Historical Review,* 42 (1973), 143–63.
23 Belohlavek, *Let the Eagle Soar,* 162–77; Tyler Dennett, *Americans in Eastern Asia* (New York: MacMillan, 1922), 128–34, 244–46.
24 Belohlavek, *Let the Eagle Soar,* 243–50; E.T. Parks, *Colombia and the United States* (Durham: Duke University Press, 1935), 178–89.
25 Belohlavek, *Let the Eagle Soar,* 90–114; Robert C. Thomas, "Andrew Jackson versus France," *Tennessee Historical Quarterly,* 35 (1976), 51–64.
26 Belohlavek, *Let the Eagle Soar,* 115–20.
27 Ibid., 121–26.
28 Belohlavek, *Let the Eagle Soar,* 214–23; George Rives, *The United States and Mexico, 1821–1848* (New York: Scribner, 1913), 234–91.
29 Belohlavek, *Let the Eagle Soar,* 224–37.

CHAPTER **6**

RETIREMENT AT THE HERMITAGE (1837–1845)

Power. The war between Andrew Jackson's allies and enemies over his use and abuse of power commanded public and political attention into the waning weeks of his administration. Thomas Hart Benton, who had personally attempted to end Old Hickory's life in a Nashville tavern almost 25 years earlier, made an impassioned plea before the Senate in January 1837, urging the repeal of that body's censure of Jackson in 1834. Reputation and right mattered in erasing from the record blame for King Andrew's single-handed destruction of the Bank of the United States. Calhoun and Clay rose to denounce the resolution, unsubtly referencing such actions as appropriate to the era of despotic Roman emperors Nero and Caligula. Clay fatalistically counted the votes, and they were not in his favor. The Kentuckian still found time for Shakespeare. "The deed is to be done," he admitted, "that foul deed, like the blood-stained hands of the guilty Macbeth, all ocean's waters will never wash out." "Proceed then," Clay implored, "like other skilled executioners, do it quickly."

Benton planned for a marathon, not a sprint, ordering a dinner of turkey, ham, wine, pickles, and hot coffee for the Democrats. Near midnight on January 16, the weary Whigs conceded, and the expunging measure passed by a vote of 24 to 19. Boos rang out in the Senate galleries, prompting Benton to yell "Bank ruffians! Bank ruffians!" and instruct the House officers to apprehend the miscreants. Both order and Jackson's honor were restored. Benton sent the pen used in the ceremony to a grateful president, who hosted a celebratory dinner for the loyal senators.[1]

One month later, on February 22, a mighty throng of men, women, and children turned out at the White House for the general's farewell gala. Many realized it would be their last opportunity to see and touch an American hero. The retiring president humbly accepted a series of gifts; a group of

New York citizens presented him with an elegant carriage made of timbers from "Old Ironsides," the *USS Constitution*. More modest and equally pleasing tributes arrived, including a simple hat handcrafted by a Brooklyn laborer. Jackson assured the workman, "I shall wear it with prouder feelings than I would a crown." The Whigs no doubt would have agreed with the appropriateness of the regal headdress.[2]

These moments of satisfaction and gratitude were compromised, however, by an antagonistic and chaotic Congress that attacked Jackson even as he prepared to depart for Nashville and the Hermitage. The issue of abolition and slavery seemed inescapable. Old Hickory had earlier in 1835 sided with Postmaster General Amos Kendall over the mailing of abolitionist literature into the South. Over 175,000 pamphlets found their way beyond the Mason–Dixon Line, where angry South Carolinians protested their arrival by seizing the literature. The president agreed with Kendall that such incendiary publications should be confiscated, unless some misguided soul actually wanted to receive it. Jackson, who often exerted the power of the chief executive and the federal government in matters related to the preservation of the Union, deferred to the southern states when the subject of slavery arose. He viewed the mailings as a plot by abolitionist elements to stir up "the horrors of a servile war."[3]

In Congress, those elements led by John Quincy Adams, continued to press for the right to present petitions advocating abolition. The House of Representatives passed a "gag rule" in May 1836, which immediately tabled any such appeals without discussion. Debate over this issue, and the denial of free speech and the right of petition, often turned confrontational and sometimes violent. Jackson and the Democrats saw little moral dimension to their opponents' arguments. They generally believed that the problem was constitutionally left to the states. Any effort at interfering with the domestic institution was really an attack on popular democracy, as well as an attempt to discredit the administration and agitate disunionist sentiment.

The unrelenting Whigs launched their own investigations into corrupt patronage practices within the administration, especially involving the Treasury Department. While these inquiries faltered, the Congress attempted to repeal the president's Specie Circular of July 1836 which had required that purchasers pay for federal land in gold or silver. An irate Jackson refused to yield, and his last official act on March 3, 1837, was a pocket veto of the measure.[4]

The Democrats could take some solace in the political state of affairs. They controlled both houses of Congress and Martin Van Buren had triumphed in the recent presidential contest. The New Yorker, mistrusted and unpopular in the South, needed Jackson's strong endorsement to attain the nomination. The party added frontier masculinity and a slave owner to the ticket by choosing Richard M. Johnson as their vice president. The Kentuckian's campaign slogan "Rumpsey dumpsey, rumpsey dumpsey, Colonel Johnson killed Tecumsey", trumpeted his supposed slaying of the Shawnee chief at the Battle of the Thames during the War of 1812.

Since the Whigs could not agree on a single candidate, aspirants ranging from Daniel Webster in New England, Hugh Lawson White and Willie P. Mangum in the South, and William Henry Harrison in the West entered the fray, hoping to divide the vote and throw the contest into the House of Representatives. The strategy failed and Van Buren secured a solid electoral margin, although he captured barely 50 percent of the popular vote.

Pity the Little Magician. On March 4, 1837, he climbed the stairs of the Capitol to take his inaugural oath as the eighth president of the United States. Accompanied and overshadowed by the presence of the Old Hero, the diminutive New Yorker could only look on as the assembled crowd once more cheered their departing champion. Jackson's Farewell Address offered a balanced commentary on the evolution of the republic with a healthy dose of caution. The nation had made significant gains towards unity, advancing democracy, and restraining the forces of privilege. However, elements existed that wanted "to excite the South against the North and the North against the South, and to force into the controversy the most delicate and exciting topics—topics upon which it is impossible that a large portion of the Union can ever speak without strong emotion . . . and the possible dissolution of the Union has at length become an ordinary and familiar subject of discussion."

Slavery had already emerged as a splintering issue, and Jackson's prescient comments about the collapse of the Union were followed by an even more troubling prediction. "If the Union is once severed, the line of separation will grow wider and wider, and the controversies which are now debated and settled in the halls of legislation will then be tried in the fields of battle and determined by the sword." Jackson might be leaving Washington filled with concern, but Van Buren soon found that he would benefit from and endure the counsel of his predecessor for the next four years.[5]

Jackson's journey home to Nashville by railroad, highway, and steamboat took almost three weeks. Along the way, he was exalted and exhausted by a series of dinners, parades, and celebrations. He was not well. Plagued by a relentless cough, swollen feet, pain in the side, and impaired vision, his health had collapsed in November 1836. A serious cold produced a fit of coughing that resulted in a serious hemorrhage. The White House doctor rushed in to deal with the situation and took even more blood—over two quarts (70 ounces)—during a two-day period. Somehow Jackson survived, living on an austere diet of milk and mush. His weakened condition required him to remain confined to the White House for the remainder of his presidency.

Arriving at the Hermitage in late March, Old Hickory settled into a routine. The homecoming was bittersweet. His son, Andrew, Jr., daughter-in-law Sarah, and their children provided Jackson with the family and care he badly needed. At nearby Poplar Grove, nephew Andrew Jackson Donelson mourned the recent loss of his wife. Emily, the surrogate first lady in the White House, had tragically died at the age of 29 after a lingering illness in December 1836. While she and Jackson suffered through an estrangement over the "petticoat affair", the breach had been healed. Emily and her children vacationed with him as recently as July at the Rip Raps, a small island at Hampton Roads, Virginia. The holiday failed to help his health, as Jackson's physical deterioration continued unabated. He had not recovered from the near-death experience in the Capitol, and a troubling fall at the Hermitage aroused concern. Persistent and acute vision and pain issues were compounded by bouts of debilitating earaches and headaches.

By 1837, the Hermitage, rebuilt after the disastrous fire three years earlier, had become a massive investment in crops, horses, buildings, and over 150 slaves. Unfortunately, Andrew had badly mismanaged the plantation, leaving his father in dire straits. The errors in judgment and resulting debts persisted, with Jackson continually cleaning up his son's financial mess. Jackson moved quickly to try to restore fiscal sanity, selling a number of horses and property in Alabama, and cutting back on the overseer's salary. Interestingly, he borrowed over $1,000 to provide legal counsel for four of his slaves accused of the murder of a fellow slave at a Christmas party. The men were found innocent, but Jackson needed to sell farmland to meet the obligation. He still enjoyed riding the property, checking on the crops, and conversing with the slaves, but sadly, his weakened condition limited his endurance and ability to spend time outdoors. Increasingly, his world narrowed to entertaining admiring strangers and friends, and writing letters of advice and encouragement to his Democratic disciples.[6]

Political, as well as personal, events clouded Jackson's horizon. Within weeks of his departure from Washington, the cotton market collapsed, creating a downward spiral that resulted in bankruptcies, foreclosures, and an overall financial malaise. The Panic of 1837, and subsequent depression, particularly affected the industrial and commercial sectors and lasted throughout the Van Buren presidency. In an era when no Federal Reserve System existed to bolster the economy, and the national government did not play a role in public relief, the Magician had no tricks up his sleeve to treat the ills plaguing the nation.

As the country drifted, the politicians blamed each other for the widespread suffering. Surely, Jackson, his Deposit Act and Specie Circular, ushered in the collapse, the Whigs argued. The Democrats retorted that greedy and speculative capitalists had abandoned gold and silver, and the resultant free flow of paper money and an overheated economy had sparked the panic. Both parties made legitimate points. The ebb and flow of worldwide demands for goods and specie could be added to the mix. The United States, increasingly reliant on global commerce and possessing little gold or silver, was vulnerable to the vagaries of a global marketplace.

Jackson could not divorce himself from the problems, economic or otherwise, of the new administration. He read newspapers religiously and stayed current on affairs in Washington. His fears and concerns prompted at least two letters a month to Van Buren offering advice. Sometimes solicited, sometimes not, Old Hickory's counsel encouraged the president to hold fast on the issue of hard money and maintain his courage on behalf of the people and against the wealthy and privileged. Jackson recommended the creation of an Independent Treasury, an institution that would house and disperse federal funds, but would not incorporate the risks of a bank. Van Buren agreed with the proposal, but could not persuade Congress to pass the measure. Secretary of War Joel Poinsett also received his share of guidance, Jackson expressing his displeasure with the slow pace of the Seminole War and the foot-dragging of the Cherokees in removal. As scholar Robert Remini emphasized, rather than fading into retirement, "Jackson continued to play an active and vigorous role in national affairs. His presence was constantly felt, especially at Democratic conventions and meetings involving policy decisions."[7]

The general struggled with periodic hemorrhaging and fading eyesight, and each time he had a bleeding episode, death seemed imminent. Perhaps in a final admission of his mortality, in July 1838 Old Hickory joined the Presbyterian Church, the faith of his beloved mother and wife. Neither his maladies, nor his beliefs prohibited Jackson from drinking. He reportedly favored Kentucky sour mash bourbon, particularly "Old Crow," but added "burnt brandy," to his beverage list. For years, Jackson had suffered from dysentery and loose bowels, and swore that a light diet of rice, milk, and coffee, plus a wine glass of the mixture of heated sugar and brandy three times a day would end one's misery—or perhaps make one oblivious to the discomfort. His travels remained limited. He mustered the financial and physical resources to attend the silver jubilee of the Battle of New Orleans on January 8, 1840. Over 30,000 gathered to parade, toast, and celebrate the Old Hero and the most glorious victory in American history.[8]

As the presidential election approached in November, the Panic of 1837 hung like an albatross around Van Buren's neck. At their rallies, the Whigs heartily chanted, "Van, Van is a used-up man!" The nation drifted slowly towards a cyclical recovery, while Washington battled over whether to create a new national bank or a less intrusive Independent Treasury.

Congress finally approved the Democratic alternative in the summer of 1840, too late to salve the economic wounds of the country or save "Matty Van's" re-election bid. In his own paternalistic manner, Jackson hovered over the process, urging the replacement of controversial Vice President Richard M. Johnson. The Kentuckian had infuriated a number of southerners by his public relationships with several slave women. Julia Chinn, an octoroon, was his common law wife and the most well known. She bore him two daughters before her untimely death of cholera in 1833. Jackson argued that the unpopular president needed a strong, experienced Democrat on the ticket, such as former Speaker of the House James K. Polk, a Tennessee slaveholder with an untarnished reputation. The party dumped Johnson, but could reach no consensus on an alternative.[9]

The Whigs shamelessly copied from the Democratic political playbook. William Henry Harrison, yet another Indian fighter from the War of 1812, teamed with former Virginia Democrat John Tyler—"Tippecanoe and Tyler, Too"—to attack the unfortunate Van Buren and hail the military hero. The "Log Cabin and Hard Cider" campaign deceptively portrayed Harrison as a man of common roots and tastes, and featured parades, banners and barbeques. A unique "Keep the ball rolling!" gimmick involved pushing a number of large paper, leather, or tin balls inscribed with campaign rhetoric from town to town to stir up Whig enthusiasm.

The homespun strategy, especially useful against the nattily dressed Van Buren from the Hudson River Valley, infuriated Jackson and drove him to the campaign trail. At the age of 73, he spoke extensively and ardently in western Tennessee, warning his listeners against the threat of a Whig-dominated government that would support both abolitionism and a rich elite at the expense of democracy and the people. Allied with English bankers, they would seek to crush the working classes. Jackson's efforts were to no avail. In the largest turnout in U.S. history (80 percent of the eligible voters participated) Harrison rolled to victory with a margin of 53 percent of the popular vote and captured the electoral ballots of 19 of 26 states. The Old Hero was disappointed, but not defeated. He lamented bitterly, but with no evidence, to Van Buren that "corruption, bribery, and fraud has been extended over the whole Union." The fight to preserve the gains of his administration had just begun.[10]

On April 3, 1841, 68-year-old William Henry Harrison died after a brief illness. He had served but one month. "Old Tip" decided to deliver his two-hour inaugural address on a chilly, windy March day without a hat or coat. He contracted a cold which devolved into pneumonia, and led to his unexpected death—the first president to succumb while in office. Jackson callously rejoiced at his demise, believing that the Whig agenda promoting a third national bank, higher tariffs, and massive internal improvements would be thwarted by new chief executive, John Tyler. Jackson was right. The Virginian was no Whig, and had been placed on the ticket only because of his shared disdain for Jackson. He deserted Old Hickory in the 1830s over the issues of states' rights and King Andrew's abuse of power, not because he embraced the Whig's economic program.

Tyler did not fail the Democrats. During the course of his administration, he repeatedly challenged Henry Clay, now in the Senate, on numerous critical issues. Veto followed veto, most importantly a devastating rejection of a bill to charter a new Bank of the United States. Tyler's alienation from the Whigs and his advocacy of states' rights principles led to correspondence and a reconciliation between the new president and Jackson. Even so, the general was unwilling to endorse Tyler in 1844, and began crafting a strategy for a Van Buren-Polk ticket for the upcoming contest. The wily Magician firmed up his support by visiting the Hermitage as part of a southern tour in the spring of 1842.[11]

Many wondered whether Jackson would survive to witness the election. His health continued its downward spiral. He suffered an apparent heart attack in the summer of 1841, and was injured when his carriage overturned in November 1843. Pain consumed him. His skeletal frame, weakened by periodic lung hemorrhages and bowel complaints, endured further damage from frequently ingested toxic concoctions containing lead (sugar of lead) and mercury (calomel). The primitive medicine of the era also gave great latitude to the crafting of dangerous patent potions. Jackson swore by "Matchless Sanative," which contained alcohol and likely opiates. To add to the misery, his son Andrew continued to mismanage money and their plantations. Andrew Jr. had purchased the Halcyon plantation in Mississippi in 1838, but crop failures there and at the Hermitage caused cash flow problems. Debts mounted, leaving Jackson in an almost desperate position. He was obliged to secure loans from friends, mortgage Halcyon and its 30 slaves, and sell a number of prized horses. Sadly, this pattern of Andrew's bungling and his father scrambling for relief repeated itself until the Old Hero's death. Andrew inherited the Hermitage and the surrounding thousand acres, but ongoing financial missteps compelled him to sell the property to the state of Tennessee within a decade of his father's burial.[12]

In spite of his personal issues, Old Hickory remained vigilant in observing both domestic and diplomatic events. Great Britain posed an ongoing challenge to the American hemispheric vision. Jackson followed the ill-fated rebellion in Canada against British rule, and border skirmishes in the northeast that threatened war between the U.S. and the Crown. Jackson was appalled with the boundary agreement between Canada and Maine negotiated by old adversary, now secretary of state, Daniel Webster. The Webster–Ashburton Treaty of 1842 gave the U.S. 7,000 out of 12,000 contested square miles of land. Jackson had some reason to complain. He had supported an arbitration offered by King William of the Netherlands in 1831, which awarded the U.S. almost a thousand *more* square miles of territory. The agreement had encountered stiff opposition within the cabinet, but also from National Republicans not eager to help build Jackson's legacy in foreign affairs. Governor Samuel Smith and the Maine legislature emerged as more ironic obstacles. South Carolina would soon move to assert its states' rights regarding the tariff, while Maine representatives used a similar argument to oppose a judgment that compromised their territorial sovereignty. Both Maine and South Carolina argued that Jackson abused the power of his office and prompted overreach by the federal government. In June 1831, the Senate rejected the King's arbitration and voted to reopen talks with Great Britain. Resolution came only a decade later in 1842 and on terms that Jackson deemed "disgraceful" and "humiliating."[13]

Old Hickory was more concerned about British ambitions in the South and West. He joined a growing number of Americans fearful that London had its imperial sights set on the jointly occupied Oregon country, Mexican-owned California, and, most importantly, the Lone Star Republic. Texas was rapidly becoming one of the most productive cotton-producing areas in the region and a gateway into the Southwest. British acquisition of any of these areas would prevent expansion westward onto valuable new farm lands and pose an ongoing security threat to the Union. Jackson had, of course, his own long-held view of continental empire, and attempted to purchase Texas. Consequently, he was delighted to learn that his old comrade, Sam Houston, the president of the republic, desired annexation.

Since 1837, the divisive debate over the expansion of slavery had stonewalled any congressional move in the direction of annexation. Jackson eagerly enlisted in the cause, acting as a conduit of information between Texas and Washington, and publicly touting the critical importance of the unification of the two republics. The forces of Manifest Destiny, the God-given right of the United States to expand across North America, argued that the question was indeed one of natural rights and security. Unfortunately for the champions of annexation, the treaty submitted by Secretary of State John C. Calhoun and considered by the Senate in 1844 became bogged down in revelations that the motivation for annexation was more likely slavery than security. On the heels of the disclosure, the Senate voted decisively (35 to 16) to reject the agreement.[14]

Slavery and Texas remained high-profile topics in the 1844 campaign. Martin Van Buren and Henry Clay, the probable choices of the Democrats and Whigs, conveniently agreed to equivocate and oppose immediate annexation. Both realized that a clear stand would alienate either the northern or southern wings of their respective parties. A distraught Jackson read Van Buren's public statement on the matter with regret. He believed that his old friend could not garner the necessary southern support to get elected, and another candidate must be found. Jackson had just the man in mind—James K. Polk. Although Polk had been Speaker of the House and governor of Tennessee, he remained nationally obscure. Jackson strategized with Polk's supporters to make him the "available man," once Van Buren's candidacy faltered at the convention. And falter it did. When Van Buren failed to obtain the needed two-thirds vote for nomination, Polk was chosen on the ninth ballot. The party platform touting the "reoccupation of Oregon and re-annexation of Texas" warmed the old soldier's heart. Jackson believed, as did many Americans, that Texas had been ceded to the U.S. as part of the Louisiana Purchase of 1803. Following the War of 1812, American diplomats made the rather dubious claim that the Rio Grande formed the western boundary of the purchase, at least until John Quincy Adams surrendered that claim in the Transcontinental Treaty of 1819. The present move to "re-annex" simply affirmed that position.

Since the Whigs selected Henry Clay as their candidate, Jackson viewed the contest as a struggle for the soul of the nation. He engaged as much as physically possible, writing letters which appeared in newspapers across the country in support of the man dubbed "Young Hickory." Polk won by the narrowest of margins. He bested Clay by only 1 percent in the popular vote, and the loss of New York in the electoral college would have turned the contest to the Whigs. Historians debate whether the presence of antislavery Liberty Party candidate James G. Birney siphoned votes from Clay in key states and gave Polk the victory. Jackson had lived to see the Democrats restored to power. "The Republic is safe," he pronounced with a genuine sense of relief.[15]

Old Hickory also survived to witness his vision of Texas annexation become a reality. In the waning days of the Tyler administration, the pro-annexation forces introduced a joint resolution that required a simple majority of both houses rather than a two-thirds vote of approval by the Senate. The narrow Senate majority was achieved only through the cooperation of three southern Whigs and was signed by the President on March 1, 1845. Jackson rejoiced, yet did not step back from the public sphere. He continued to convey his views on matters of policy and personnel to his Tennessee disciple. Jackson's last letter urged Polk to look into previous financial wrongdoing in the Treasury Department of the Tyler administration. The president pleased his mentor with classically Jacksonian views on domestic and foreign affairs, but disappointed him with questionable dismissals and appointments to office. Young Hickory would be his own man.

In his final months, Jackson was bloated by dropsy, a condition in which the cavities of the body are flooded with fluid. Doctors drained his abdomen to relieve the pain. Unable to lie down, he could barely move from his bed to a nearby armchair. Tortured by decades of accumulative disease, cures, bullets, and bleeding, he simply gave out. Preparing for the end, Jackson expressed the concern that "heaven will be no heaven if I do not meet my wife there." Death came quietly on the evening of June 8, 1845. Surrounded by sobbing family and friends, his final words were a gentle admonition about the hereafter, "I want to meet you all in heaven, both black and white . . . Do not cry, be good children and we will all meet in heaven." The apocryphal story circulated about a friend asking "Uncle Alfred," a long-time slave at the Hermitage, whether Jackson was now in heaven. The old man responded, "General Jackson will get into heaven if he wants to."

With age, Old Hickory had mellowed and become more religious. The younger, hard-edged Jackson, however, was not averse to swearing, among his favorite expressions the rather tame "By the Eternal!" Rachel's cherished parrot "Poll" was still alive, and was present at Jackson's open-casket funeral at the Hermitage. The bird took the opportunity to repeat at loud volume every curse word and obscenity he had learned over almost two decades, perhaps from the master of the house. The three thousand in attendance were so stunned by the prolonged display that the minister was obliged to have "Poll" forcibly removed from the building. One wonders whether Jackson would have been similarly troubled, or perhaps amused, at the parrot's tribute.

Over the next several weeks, more somber and elaborate ceremonies were held across the country in towns large and small in honor of the Old Hero. Processions in New York, Baltimore, and Philadelphia drew huge crowds eager to pay their respects to a symbol of the age. In Washington, government offices closed, and the president ordered the military to wear symbols of mourning for six months. Incredibly, Andrew Jackson really was mortal, and the nation would be a different place in his absence. Loved and hated, revered and despised, his legacy remained controversial but undeniable.[16]

NOTES

1 Robert Remini, *Andrew Jackson and the Course of American Democracy 1833–1845* (New York: Harper and Row, 1984), 377–81, Jon Meacham, *American Lion: Andrew Jackson in the White House* (New York: Random House, 2008), 335–37, Donald B. Cole *The Presidency of Andrew Jackson* (Lawrence: University Press of Kansas, 1993), 264–66.
2 Remini, *American Democracy*, 404–05.
3 William Lee Miller, *Arguing about Slavery: John Quincy Adams and the Great Battle in the United States Congress* (New York: Random House, 1995), 102–03.
4 Ibid., 139–49; Remini, *American Democracy*, 406–12; Meacham, *American Lion*, 304–06.
5 Sean Wilentz, *The Rise of Democracy: From Jefferson to Lincoln* (New York: WW Norton, 2005), 446–55; Jackson Farewell Address, March 4, 1837, Richardson, *Messages and Papers*, III, 292–96.

6. Remini, *American Democracy,* 420–28, 258, 369–70, 432–33; H.W. Brands, *Andrew Jackson: His Life and Times* (New York: Anchor Books, 2006), 532–34; Mark R. Cheathem, *Andrew Jackson: Southerner* (Baton Rouge: Louisiana State University Press, 2013), 182–88.
7. Wilentz, *Rise of Democracy,* 457–65; Remini, *American Democracy,* 427–37, 440; Brands, *Andrew Jackson,* 534–35.
8. Remini, *American Democracy,* 452–60.
9. Wilentz, *Rise of Democracy,* 448.
10. Ibid., 493–507; Remini, *American Democracy,* 464–70; Brands, *Andrew Jackson,* 537–40.
11. Remini, *American Democracy,* 462–71, Wilentz, *Rise of Democracy,* 521–26.
12. Remini, *American Democracy,* 453, 472–83, Brands, *Andrew Jackson,* 541–44.
13. John M. Belohlavek, *Let the Eagle Soar!: The Foreign Policy of Andrew Jackson.* (Lincoln: University of Nebraska Press, 1985), 60–71; Remini, *American Democracy,* 481–82.
14. Joel Silbey, *Storm over Texas: The Annexation Controversy and the Road to Civil War* (New York: Oxford University Press, 2005), 39–50; Remini, *American Democracy,* 490–96.
15. Walter R. Borneman, *Polk: The Man Who Transformed the Presidency* (New York: Random House, 2008), 94–128; Remini, *American Democracy,* 495–508.
16. Ibid., 512–29; James Parton, *The Life of Andrew Jackson* (New York: Mason Brothers, 1860), III, 678–79.

CHAPTER 7

THE JACKSON LEGACY

Principle

Few presidents have been as revered and vilified as Andrew Jackson. Into the twenty-first century, the mere mention of his name in historical circles is certain to draw emotional outbursts of admiration or disdain. In the public realm, while the Hermitage remains the third most visited historic presidential mansion (after Washington's Mount Vernon and Jefferson's Monticello), debate continues over whether Old Hickory's image should be removed from the twenty dollar bill. This complicated man, who championed American democracy and believed in the will of the people as few leaders before or after him, also owned slaves and relocated Indians. He was indeed a man of principle and prejudice.

After the War of 1812, individual states revised their Revolutionary-era constitutions and empowered most white males with the ballot. Jackson did not create this vastly extended voting body, but he advanced and organized its potential power. Elites who had previously chosen candidates and determined elections now faced a rising, largely agrarian class determined to craft its own future. Over time, numerous urban working men also joined this coalition to constitute a majoritarian rather than a representative democracy. Jackson broadly referred to these "working" or "laboring" classes, the mechanics and farmers, as sovereign. Old Hickory, however, believed in the principle of their participation in the process, and talked incessantly about their right to rule the republic. Certainly, not all these new voters believed in the Jacksonian agenda; many joined the National Republican or Whig camps.

The general often warned Americans about backsliding into an era when men of wealth, privilege, and education made decisions for the people.

Special interests had combined with the greedy and unethical to pervert the American political system. For Jackson, the widespread contamination reached into too many sectors of national politics and the economy. Crooked contracts and bribes siphoned off federal dollars needed for essential services and to pay off the federal debt. Jackson entered office in 1829 with a reform agenda. Not only would he root out the fraudulent, but he intended to reform the electoral process; an issue made abundantly clear by the corrupt bargain of 1824–1825. Jackson urged the direct election of the U.S. president, senators, and judges, elimination of the electoral college, and limiting the chief executive to a single term. He failed. None of these measures was realized in his lifetime, and only one (the direct election of senators through the seventeenth amendment passed in 1913) was ever implemented. His advocacy, however, speaks to a commitment to the principle of expanding the power of the people in choosing their leaders at many levels.

Old Hickory believed in the principle of expressing the voice of the populace through grass-roots mass political parties. He formed an impressive coalition, started by his western friends, the Nashville Junto, and strengthened by personages such as Thomas Hart Benton, John C. Calhoun, and Martin Van Buren. The forces around the Tennessean fused into the Jacksonian Democratic Party. While his many lieutenants played a major role in providing sage counsel, shifting his views, and crafting various documents, there was no doubt who was in charge. Jackson bore the responsibility for both good and bad personnel choices and policy decisions. The Democrats took techniques pioneered by the Jeffersonian Republicans of a generation earlier—parades, picnics, barbeques, and newspapers—and moved them to a more sophisticated level. In the prior decade, the states created the voter potential by extending the ballot, but the Jacksonians and their opponents energized that electorate.

He was Old Hickory, the first president with a nickname, one that reminded the masses of his sacrifice to the nation on the battlefield. Jackson first declared the principle that the man in the White House represented *all* of the American people. This notion of a popular presidency and challenge to the primacy of Congress was not well received. Jackson pressed on, repeatedly defying the legislative branch with his vetoes. What his enemies viewed as abuse of executive authority, his supporters saw as bold action, professing the voice of the people through the chief executive. Since the president was co-equal with the other branches of government, Jackson felt comfortable disputing congressional laws and Supreme Court decisions.

Jackson took the power of the office to new levels, asserting the principle not only of the veto, but in advocating rotation in public appointments and audaciously replacing virtually his entire cabinet in one swift stroke.

Since Old Hickory surrounded himself with the first informal Kitchen Cabinet of advisors; the forced resignations of his formal cabinet in 1831 and the continuity of their successors mattered less than it might have to Madison or Monroe. While frequent change no doubt affected the operation of the government's departments, Jackson's inner circle often carried more weight in the decision-making process.

Did Andrew Jackson believe in the soft hand of states' rights or a robust national government? In fact, the answer is both. He strongly endorsed Jefferson's viewpoint of limiting the power of Washington, and emphasizing the ability of the states to make decisions that would benefit the interests of their own constituents. Like the Virginian, Jackson soon learned that when national interests became paramount, the insular agenda of the state must be put aside. Similarly, situations demanded that the president assert his authority, with or without the support of Congress. Jefferson the philosopher wrestled with these tensions much more than Jackson the pragmatist. While his core beliefs remained steady, Jackson adopted hard stands on issues relating to the permanence of the Union and the power of his office.

The parochial Jackson also held a world view. His internationalist foreign policy fostered the principle of respect for the American fleet and flag. He demanded the safety of U.S. commercial vessels on the high seas and garnered reparations for past wrongdoing by various European powers. Missions were dispatched to Latin America, the Middle East, and Asia to foster access to trade and markets. He promoted the principle of a U.S.-dominated North America, scheming and planning to add territory from Florida to California. Failures often matched accomplishments, but the vision and goals were remarkable for a boy who grew up in the Waxhaws of Carolina.

Prejudice

Andrew Jackson struggled with the Christian notion of forgiveness. Over a lifetime, he developed an extensive list of personal and political enemies. For Jackson, who viewed himself as the paternalistic father of an extended family, a political party, and a nation, he easily justified the intersection of the two camps. As his tears flowed at Rachel's funeral, the distraught husband declared, "In the presence of this dear saint I can and do forgive all my enemies. But those vile wretches who have slandered her must look to God for mercy."[1]

Jackson blamed the stress of a presidential campaign filled with base charges and sexual innuendo for his wife's premature death. Henry Clay, an old political adversary, received the lion's share of the censure. Soon thereafter, the administration imploded over the "petticoat affair", an unnecessary and disastrous scenario that tore at the fabric of the new Democratic Party.

Jackson identified the culprit as his own vice president, John C. Calhoun. No wonder that Jackson was later reported to have made the statement, "My only two regrets in life are that I did not hang Calhoun and shoot Clay." Whether Old Hickory actually said those words is largely irrelevant; he was apt to believe them. Jackson's rhetoric was often powerful and extreme. His statement to Van Buren about the Bank of the U.S. trying to kill him was accurate. The National Republicans most certainly attempted to use the institution as a wedge issue to destroy Jackson and his candidacy in 1832. He assumed that the opposition represented the privileged classes who had set about to undermine the welfare of the American people and their rising democracy to benefit the moneyed elites.

His prejudices were both racial and national. As a southerner and westerner, Jackson never considered notions of equality regarding African Americans or Indians. His republic was destined by God for a special place in the world, an American exceptionalism, and that place would be achieved through the intelligence and energy of white men and their families. Blacks functioned in a vital role as slave labor to support growth, but not to compete as free men. Slaves should be faithful, disciplined, and hardworking. In turn, that loyalty should be rewarded with kindness, accompanied by proper food, clothing, and housing. They should be treated well by their masters, but the whip was an omnipresent consequence for bad behavior, and freedom was never in the equation. Jackson was that master. Native Americans garnered respect from Jackson. While he saw them as inferior, even savages, he admired their courage and wanted to preserve their way of life in the West. As an obstacle to white advancement and the fulfillment of the American agricultural dream, however, they had to make way for a superior civilization.

Jackson had little use for foreigners. One of the country's most parochial and least travelled presidents, he journeyed only as far as New Orleans and Boston. He never left the United States, except for his venture into Spanish Florida in the First Seminole War, and possessed neither formal education nor language skills. These limitations did not prohibit the general from developing his own set of prejudices based on impression and experience. He thoroughly mistrusted Europeans, particularly the French and Spanish. French obstinacy and double-dealing concerning the spoliations claims over a period of years convinced Jackson of their lack of integrity. Of course, Jackson acquired his initial impressions of the Spanish along the western frontier and in Florida, solidified by his dealings during his brief tenure as governor in 1821. Latin Americans, of mixed race and predominantly Spanish in language, likewise commanded little deference. Possessing both Texas and California, Mexico was viewed not as a friendly neighbor, but as another impediment to American progress. The British ranked slightly higher in his estimation, based on their culture, history, and power. Jackson never forgot, however, the scar on his forehead and the impact of the Revolution on his family. As an adult, he suspected their imperial intentions, convinced that the Crown wanted to obstruct the continental destiny of the U.S. and retain power in the Americas for itself.

Jackson was violent, compassionate, brutal, caring, insensitive, and consummately patriotic. Some of his actions were predictable, many others surprised even his friends. From bleeding revolutionary farm boy to Nashville plantation aristocrat, Jackson embodied the antebellum dream. The first president to come from common roots, he prided himself on his understanding of the people. They rarely disappointed him.

This volume is intended to raise questions about the multi-faceted nature of Andrew Jackson and help explain why the man as general and president is endlessly controversial. He remains contradictory and sometimes hard to understand. Was he complex in his simplicity or perhaps simple in his complexity? In 2014, a national survey of political scientists ranked him within the top ten of American presidents—in the great category—while simultaneously suggesting that he is among the most overrated. The debate over Old Hickory's stature continues unabated, but his importance in American history appears firmly in place.[2]

Notes

1 Marquis James, *The Life of Andrew Jackson* (New York: Bobbs–Merrill, 1938), 174.
2 Sean Wilentz, *Andrew Jackson,* (New York: Times Books, 205), 150–66, Buell, *Andrew Jackson,* II, 363, American Political Science Association Survey, *Washington Post,* February 16, 2015.

PART II

DOCUMENTS

1 Andrew Jackson Challenges Charles Dickinson
   to a Duel: June 14, 1806   123
2 Campaign Song "The Hunters of Kentucky" (1828)   125
3 Jackson's First Inauguration: March 4, 1829   127
4 Jackson and Indian Removal: December 6, 1830   129
5 "Rats Leaving a Falling House", Cartoon (1831)   132
6 Jackson and the Bank Veto: July 10, 1832   134
7 Jackson on Nullification: December 10, 1832   137
8 "Henry Clay Sews Up Jackson's Mouth", Cartoon (1834)   139
9 Jackson's Farewell Address: March 4, 1837   141
10 Jackson Comments on Texas Annexation: February 12, 1843 143

DOCUMENT 1

Jackson Challenges Charles Dickinson to a Duel

JUNE 14, 1806

Andrew Jackson loved horses and gambling. He became embroiled in a quarrel over money owed him by Captain Joseph Ervin as payment of a debt from a canceled race in Nashville. Charles Dickinson, Ervin's son-in-law, and friend Thomas Swann became involved, and Dickinson branded Jackson "a worthless scoundrel, a poltroon and a coward." The deadly duel took place in Kentucky on Friday, May 30, 1806.

Dear Sir:

Your conduct and expressions relative to me of late have been of such a nature and so insulting that it requires and shall have my notice.

Insults may be given by men, and of such a kind, that they must be noticed and treated with the respect due a gentleman, although as in the present instance you do not merit it.

You have, to disturb my quiet, industriously excited Thomas Swann to quarrel with me, which involved the peace and harmony of society for a while.

You on the 10th of January wrote me a very insulting letter, left this country, caused this letter to be delivered after you had been gone some days, and viewing yourself in safety from the contempt I held you in—have now in the press a piece more replete with blackguard abuse than any of your other productions. You are pleased to state that you would have noticed me in a different way, but my cowardice, would have found a pretext to evade that satisfaction if it had been called for.

I hope for your courage will be an ample security to me that I will obtain speedily that satisfaction due me for the insults offered, and in the way, my friend who hands you this will point out—he waits upon you for that purpose and with your friend will enter into immediate arrangements for this purpose.

I am,
   Andrew Jackson

Source

Nashville *Impartial Review or Cumberland Repository*, June 14, 1806 in

Andrew Burstein, *The Passions of Andrew Jackson* (New York: A.A. Knopf, 2003), 58.

DOCUMENT 2

Campaign Song "The Hunters Of Kentucky"

1821

Massachusetts-born Samuel Woodworth penned this song in 1821. Though best known for his poem "The Old Oaken Bucket," Woodworth's light, humorous tribute to Jackson, Kentucky riflemen, and the American victory at the battle of New Orleans was widely sung in the decade, and became the primary Jacksonian campaign song in 1828.

Ye gentlemen and ladies fair, who grace this famous city,
Just listen, if you've time to spare, while I rehearse a ditty;
And for the opportunity consider yourselves quite lucky,
For 'tis not often that you see a hunter from Kentucky.

Oh, Kentucky! The hunters of Kentucky.

We are a hardy free-born race, each man to fear a stranger,
Whate'er the game we join chase, despising toil and danger;
And if a daring foe annoys us, whate'er his strength and forces,
We'll show him that Kentucky boys are alligator horses.

Oh, Kentucky! The hunters of Kentucky.

I s'pose you've read in the prints, how Packenham attempted,
To make Old Hickory Jackson wince, but soon his schemes repented;
For we with rifles ready cocked, thought such occasion lucky,
And soon around the general flocked the hunters of Kentucky.

You've heard, I s'pose how New Orleans is famed for wealth and beauty,
There's girls of every hue, it seems, from snowy white to sooty,
So Packenham he made his brags, if he in fight was lucky,
He'd have their girls and cotton bags in spite of old Kentucky.

But Jackson he was wide awake, and wasn't scared at trifles,
For well he knew what aim we take with our Kentucky rifles;
So he led us down to cypress swamp, the ground was low and mucky,
There stood John Bull in martial pomp, and here was old Kentucky.

A bank was raised to hide our breast, not that we thought of dying,
But then we always like to rest unless the game is flying;
Behind it stood our little force, none wished it to be greater,
For every man was half a horse and half an alligator.

They did not let our patience tire, before they showed their faces—
We did not choose to waste our fire, so snugly kept our places;
But when so near to see them wink, we thought it time to stop 'em
And t'would have done you good I think to see Kentuckians drop 'em.

They found at last twas vain to fight, where lead was all their booty,
And so they wisely took to flight, and left us all our beauty,
And now if danger e'er annoys, remember what our trade is,
Just send for us Kentucky boys, and we'll protect your ladies.

Source

Samuel Woodworth, "The Hunters of Kentucky," 1821.

DOCUMENT **3**

JACKSON'S FIRST INAUGURATION

MARCH 4, 1829

Margaret Bayard Smith, the 50-year-old wife of prominent Washington newspaper editor Samuel Smith, was a keen observer of capital society. Over decades, she had attended numerous White House gatherings, none rivaling what she witnessed in March 1829. Many of her class anticipated and feared the new democracy of Andrew Jackson, and were shocked at what they observed.

I will not anticipate, but will give you an account of the inauguration in mere detail. The whole of the preceding day, immense crowds were coming into the city from all parts, lodgings could not be obtained, and the newcomers had to go to Georgetown, which soon overflowed, and others had to go to Alexandria. I was told the Avenue and adjoining streets were so crowded on Tuesday afternoon that it was difficult to pass.

A national salute was fired early in the morning, and ushered in March 4. By 10 o'clock the Avenue was crowded with carriages of every description, from, the splendid baronet and coach, down to wagons and carts, filled with women and children, some in finery and some in rags, for it was the people's President, and all would see him, the men all walked. . . .

The day was . . . delightful, the scene animating; so we walked backwards and forward, at every turn meeting some new acquaintance and stopping to talk and shake hands. . . . We continued promenading here until three, returned home unable to stand, and threw ourselves on the sofa.

Someone came and informed us the crowd before the President's house was so far lessened that thought we might enter. This time we effected our purpose. But what a scene did we witness. The majesty of the people had disappeared, and a rabble, a mob, of boys, Negroes, women, and children—scrambling, fighting, romping. What a pity. What a pity! No arrangements had been made, no police officers placed on duty, and the whole house had been inundated by the rabble mob. We came too late.

The President, after having been literally nearly pressed to death and almost suffocated and torn to pieces by the people in their eagerness to shake hands with Old Hickory, had retreated through the back way, or south front, and had escaped to his lodgings at Gadsby's. Cut glass and china the amount of several thousand dollars had been broken in the struggle to get the refreshments. Punch and other articles had been carried out in tubs and buckets, but had it been in hogsheads it would have been insufficient; ice creams and cake and lemonade for 20,000 people for it is said that number were there, though I think the estimate exaggerated. Ladies fainted, men were seen with bloody noses, and such a scene of confusion took place as is impossible to describe; those who got in could not get out by the door again but had to scramble out of windows.

At one time, the President, who had retreated and retreated until he was pressed against the wall, could only be secured by a number of gentlemen forming round him and making a kind of barrier of their own bodies; and the pressure was so great that Colonel Bomford, who was one, said that at one time he was afraid they should have been pushed down or on the President. It was then the windows were thrown open and the torrent found an outlet, which otherwise might have proved fatal.

The concourse had not been anticipated and therefore not provided against. Ladies and gentlemen only had been expected at this levee, not the people *en masse*. But it was the people's day, and the people's President, and the people would rule. God grant that one day or other the people do not put down all rule and rulers. I fear, enlightened freemen as they are, they will be found, as they have been found in all ages and countries where they get the power in their hands, that of all tyrants, they are the most ferocious, cruel, and despotic. The noisy and disorderly rabble in the President's house brought to my mind descriptions I had read of the mobs in the Tuileries and at Versailles. I expect to hear the carpets and furniture are ruined; the streets were muddy, and these guests all went thither on foot.

Source

Margaret Bayard Smith, *The First Forty Years of Washington Society*, Gaillard Hunt, ed. (New York: Charles Scribner's Sons, 1906), 290–98.

DOCUMENT 4

JACKSON AND INDIAN REMOVAL

DECEMBER 6, 1830

Andrew Jackson had advocated the removal of Eastern Indians beyond the Mississippi River for over a decade. His election and the Democratic House and Senate majorities gave the party the opportunity to promote such legislation. In this message to Congress, Jackson justified the Removal Act of May 1830 on the grounds that the benign policy economically and culturally benefitted both Indians and whites, and provided greater border security for the nation.

It gives me great pleasure to announce to Congress that the benevolent policy of the government, steadily pursued for nearly thirty years, in relation to the removal of the Indians beyond the white settlement is approaching a happy consummation. Two important tribes have accepted the provision made for their removal at the last session of Congress, and it is believed that their example will induce the remaining tribes also to seek the same obvious advantages.

The consequences of a speedy removal will be important to the United States, to individual states, and to the Indians themselves. The pecuniary advantages which it promises to the govern are the least of its recommendations. It puts to an end all possible danger of collision between the authorities of the general and state governments on account of the Indians. It will place a dense and civilized population in large tracts of country now occupied by a few savage hunters. By opening the whole territory between Tennessee on the north and Louisiana on the south to the settlement of the whites, it will incalculably strengthen the southwestern frontier and render the adjacent states strong enough to repel future invasions without remote aid. It will relieve the whole state of Mississippi and the western part of Alabama of Indian occupancy, and enable those states to advance rapidly in population, wealth, and power.

It will separate the Indians from immediate contact with settlements of whites; free them from the power of the states; and enable them to pursue happiness in their own way and under their own crude institutions; will retard the progress of decay, which is lessening their numbers, and perhaps cause them gradually, under the protection of the government and through the influence of good counsel, to cast off their savage habits and become an interesting, civilized, and Christian community. These consequences, some of them so certain and the rest so probable, make the complete execution of the plan sanctioned by Congress at their last session an object of much solicitude.

Toward the aborigines of the country no one can indulge a more friendly feeling than myself, or would go further in attempting to reclaim them from their wandering habits and make them a happy, prosperous people. I have endeavored to impress upon them my own solemn convictions of the duties and powers of the general government in relation to the state authorities. For the justice of the laws passed by the states within the scope of their reserved powers they are not responsible to this government. As individuals we may entertain and express opinions of their acts, but as a government we have as little right to control them as have to prescribe laws for other nations.

The present policy of the government is but a continuation of the same progressive change by a milder process. The tribes which occupied the countries now constituting the Eastern states were annihilated or have melted away to make room for the whites. The waves of population and civilization are rolling westward, and we now propose to acquire the countries occupied by red men of the South and West by a fair exchange, and at the expense of the United States, to send them to a land where their existence may be prolonged and perhaps made perpetual.

Doubtless it will be painful to leave the graves of their fathers; but what do they more than our ancestors did or than our children are now doing? To better their condition in an unknown land our forefathers left all that was dear in earthly objects. Our children by thousands yearly leave the land of their birth to seek new homes in distant regions. Does humanity weep at these painful separations from everything, animate and inanimate, with which the young hearty has become entwined? Far from it.

It is rather a source of joy that our country affords scope where our young population may range unconstrained in body or in mind, developing the power and faculties of man in their highest perfection. Can it be cruel in this government when, by events wit cannot control, the Indian is made discontented in his ancient home to purchase his lands, to give him a new and extensive territory, to pay the expense of his removal, and support him a year in his new abode? How many thousands of our own people would gladly embrace the opportunity of removing to the West on such conditions? If the offers made to the Indians were extended to them, they would be hailed with gratitude and joy.

Source

Andrew Jackson, message to Congress, December 6, 1830, James Richardson, ed. *A Compilation of the Messages and Papers of the Presidents, 1789–1897*, (Washington: Government Printing Office, 1896–1899), II, 500–29.

DOCUMENT 5

"Rats Leaving a Falling House"

1831

This cartoon depicts an exhausted, white-haired Jackson sitting in a collapsing chair while the "rats"—cabinet members John Eaton, John Branch, Martin Van Buren, and Samuel Ingham—flee the scene. A winged jackass sits on the Altar of Reform. The altar and the column behind are falling over, reflecting "Public confidence in the stability of this administration." The scene follows the Eaton Affair and the resignation of the cabinet. Note that Jackson places his foot on Van Buren's tail to restrain him.

Source

Edward W. Clay (from the original) in the Library of Congress

DOCUMENT 6

JACKSON AND THE BANK VETO

JULY 10, 1832

Jackson's duel with Bank of the United States president Nicholas Biddle peaked in July 1832 with this monumental veto of the re-charter measure. The president had numerous economic, political, and constitutional objections to the bank, which he defined in this statement to both Congress and the American people. More than the veto of a single bill, it was a critical statement of executive authority and a request for a vote of confidence from the populace, heading into the fall elections.

The bill entitled "to modify and continue" the act entitled "an act to incorporate the subscribers to the Bank of the United States" was presented to me on the 4th July instant. Having considered it with that solemn regard to the principles of the Constitution which the day was calculated to inspire, and come to the conclusion that it ought not to become a law, I herewith return it to the Senate, in which it originated, with my objections. . . .

The present corporate body, denominated the president, directors, and company of the Bank of the United States, will have existed at the time this act is intended to take effect twenty years. It enjoys exclusive privilege of banking under the authority of the general government, a monopoly of its favor and support, and, as a necessary consequence, almost a monopoly of the foreign and domestic exchange. . . .

Of the twenty-five directors of this bank, five are chosen by the government and twenty by the citizen stockholders. From all voice in these elections the foreign stockholders are excluded by the charter. In proportion, therefore, as the stock is transferred to foreign holders the extent of the suffrage in the choice of directors is curtailed. Already is almost a third of the stock in foreign hands and not represented in elections. It is constantly passing out of the country, and this act will accelerate its departure. The entire control of the institution would necessarily fall into the hands of a few citizen stockholders, and the ease with which the object would be accomplished would be a temptation to designing men to secure that control in their own hands by monopolizing the remaining stock. There is danger that a president and directors would then be able to elect themselves year after year, and without responsibility or control, manage the whole concerns of the bank during the existence of its charter. It is easy to conceive that great evils to our country and its institutions might flow from such a concentration of power in the hands of a few men irresponsible to the people.

Is there no danger to our liberty and independence in a bank that in its nature has so little to bind it to our country? . . . If we must have a bank with private stockholders, every consideration of sound policy and every impulse of American feeling admonishes that it should be purely American. . . .

By its silence, considered in connection with the decision of the Supreme Court in the case of McCulloch against the state of Maryland, this act takes from the states the power to tax a portion of the banking business carried within their limits, in subversion of one of the strongest barriers which secured them against federal encroachments. Banking, like farming, manufacturing, or any other occupation or profession, is a business. . . .

The bank is professedly established as an agent of the executive branch of the government, and its constitutionality is maintained on that ground. Neither upon the propriety of present action nor upon the provisions of this act was the executive consulted. It has had no opportunity to say that it neither needs nor wants an agent clothed with such powers and favored by such exemptions. There is nothing in its legitimate functions which makes it necessary or proper. Whatever interest or influence, whether public or private, has given birth to this act, it cannot be found either in the wishes or necessities of the Executive Department, by which present action is deemed premature, and the powers conferred upon its agent not only unnecessary but dangerous to the government and the country.

It is to be regretted that the rich and powerful too often bend the acts of government to their selfish purposes. Distinctions in society will always exist under every just government. Equality of talents, of education, or of wealth cannot be produced by human institutions . . . everyman is equally entitled to protection by law; but when the laws undertake to add to these natural and just advantages artificial distinctions, to grant titles, gratuities, and exclusive privileges, to make the rich richer and the potent more powerful, the humble members of society—the farmers, mechanics, and laborers—who have neither the time nor the means of security like favors to themselves have a right to complain of the injustice of their government. There are no necessary evils in government. Its evils exist only in its abuses. . . .

SOURCE

Richardson, ed., *Messages and Papers of the Presidents,* II, 576–91.

DOCUMENT 7

JACKSON ON NULLIFICATION

DECEMBER 10, 1832

In response to South Carolina's nullification of the tariffs of 1828 and 1832, Jackson delivered a firm, unequivocal statement to the people of the state regarding his views of the constitutionality of their protest, and the consequences if they carried out their intentions. Jackson emphasizes the perpetual nature of the Union, the supremacy of federal law, and his willingness to use force to derail any plans for disregard of the law or secession.

Whereas, a convention assembled in the state of South Carolina have passed an ordinance by which they declare that the several acts and parts of acts of the Congress of the United States purporting to be laws for the imposing of duties on the importation of foreign commodities and now having actual operation and effect within the United States, and more especially, two acts for the same purpose passed on the 29th of May, 1828, and on the 14th of July, 1832, are unauthorized by the Constitution of the United States, and violate the true meaning and intent thereof, and are null and void and no law, nor binding on the citizens of the state or its officers; and by the said ordinance it is further declared to be unlawful for any of the constituted authorities of the state or of the United States to enforce the payment of the duties imposed by the said acts within the same state, and that it is the duty of the legislature to pass such laws as may be necessary to give full effect to the said ordinance....

I consider the power to annul a law of the United States, assumed by one state, incompatible with the existence of the Union, contradicted expressly by the letter of the Constitution, unauthorized by its spirit, inconsistent with every principle on which it was founded and destructive of the great object for which it was formed. . . .

Our Constitution does not contain the absurdity of giving power to make laws and another to resist them. The sages whose memory will always be reverenced have given us a practical, and, as they hoped, a permanent constitutional compact. The father of his country did not affix his revered name to so palpable an absurdity. Nor did the states, when they severally ratified it, do so under the impression that a veto on the laws of the United States was reserved to them or that they could exercise it by implication. Search the debates in all their conventions, examine the speeches of the most zealous opposers of federal authority, look at the amendments that were proposed; they are all silent—not a syllable made to correct the explicit supremacy given to the laws of the Union over those of the states, or to show that implication, as is now contended, could defeat it. . . .

Every law, then, for raising revenue, according to the South Carolina ordinance, may be rightfully annulled unless it be so framed as no law ever will or can be framed. Congress have a right to pass laws for raising revenue and each state has a right to oppose their execution—two rights directly opposed to each other; and yet is this absurdity supposed to be contained in an instrument drawn for the express purpose of avoiding collisions between the states and the general government by an assembly of the most enlightened statesmen and purest patriots ever embodied for a similar purpose. . . .

The states severally have not retained their entire sovereignty. It has been shown that in becoming parts of a nation, not members of a league, they surrendered many of their essential parts of sovereignty. The right to make treaties, declare war, levy taxes, exercise judicial and legislative powers were all of them functions of a sovereign power. The states, then, for all these important purposes, were no longer sovereign. The allegiance of their citizens was transferred, in the first instance, to the government of the United States; they became American citizens and owed obedience to the Constitution of the United States and to laws made in conformity with the powers it vested in Congress. . . .

Disunion by armed force is treason. Are you really ready to incur its guilt? If you are, on the heads of the instigators of the act be the dreadful consequences; on their heads be the dishonor, but on yours may fall the punishment. On your unhappy state will inevitably fall all the evils of the conflict you force upon the government of your country. It cannot accede to the mad project of disunion, of which you would be the first victims. Its first magistrate cannot, if he would, avoid the performance of his duty. . . .

Source

Richardson, ed., *Messages and Papers of the Presidents*, II, 640–656.

DOCUMENT **8**

"HENRY CLAY SEWS UP JACKSON'S MOUTH", CARTOON

1834

"Jackson's veto of the re-charter of the Bank of the United States and ensuing removal of federal deposits without the authority of Congress prompted a measure of censure by the Senate in 1834. The cartoon "Plain Sewing Done Here"—"Symptoms of a Locked Jaw"—depicts Whig Senator Henry Clay shutting up the president by sewing his mouth shut. Clay quotes from Shakespeare's *Hamlet*, "Might stop a hole, keep the wind away."

Source

David Claypool Johnson, illustrator, Library of Congress

DOCUMENT 9

JACKSON'S FAREWELL ADDRESS

MARCH 4, 1837

Jackson dedicated a small portion of his Farewell Address to the issues of Indians and foreign affairs. His major and extended focus was on the constitutional nature of the republic, and dire warnings about the dangers posed by the forces of disunion, around the issue of slavery, and the threat posed by a national bank and paper money.

The States which had so long been retarded in their improvement by the Indian tribes residing in their midst of them are at length relieved from the evil, and this unhappy race—the original dwellers in our land—are now placed in a situation where we may well hope that they will share in the blessings of civilization and be saved from that degradation and destruction to which they were rapidly hastening while they remained in the states; and while the safety and comfort of our own citizens have been greatly promoted by their removal, the philanthropist will rejoice that the remnant of that ill-fated race has been at length placed beyond the reach of injury or oppression, and that the paternal care of the General Government will hereafter watch over them and protect them.

If we turn to our relations with foreign powers, we find our condition equally gratifying.... Difficulties of old standing have been surmounted by friendly discussion and the mutual desire to be just, and the claims of our citizens, which have been long withheld, have at length been acknowledged and adjusted and satisfactory arrangements made for their final payment; and with a limited, and I trust temporary exception, our relations with every foreign power are now of the most friendly character, our commerce continually expanding, and our flag respected in every quarter of the world. . . .

We behold systematic efforts publicly made to sow the seeds of discord between different parts of the United States and to place party divisions directly upon geographical distinctions; to excite South against the North and the North against the South, and to force into the controversy the most delicate and exciting topics—topics upon which it is impossible that a large portion of the Union can ever speak without strong emotion. . . . the possible dissolution of the Union has at length become an ordinary and familiar subject of discussion. Has the warning voice of Washington been forgotten, or have designs already been formed to sever the Union?

What have you to gain by division and dissension? Delude not yourselves with the belief that a breach once made may be afterwards repaired. If the Union is once severed, the line of separation will grow wider and wider, and the controversies which are now debated and settled in the halls of legislation will then be tried in fields of battle and determined by the sword. . . . The first line of separation would not last for a single generation, new fragments would be torn off, new leaders would spring up, and this great and glorious Republic would soon be broken into a multitude of petty states, without commerce, without credit, jealous of one another, armed for mutual aggression, loaded with taxes to pay armies and leaders, seeking aid against each other from foreign powers, insulted and trampled upon by the nations of Europe, until, harassed with conflicts and humbled and debased in spirit, they would be ready to submit to the absolute dominion of any military adventurer and to surrender their liberty for the sake of repose. . . .

Recent events have proved that the paper-money system of this country may be used as an engine to undermine your free institutions, and those who desire to engross all the power in the hands of the few and to govern by corruption or force are aware of its power and prepared to employ it. . . . It is one of the serious evils of our present system of banking that it enables one class of society—and that by no means a numerous one—by its control over the currency, to act injuriously upon the interest of all the others and to exercise more than its just proportion of influence in political affairs.

My own race is nearly run; advanced age and failing health warn me that before long I must pass beyond the reach of human events and cease to feel the vicissitudes of human affairs. I thank God that my life has been spent in a land of liberty and that He has given me a heart to love my country with the affection of a son. And filled with gratitude for your constant and unwavering kindness, I bid you a last and affectionate farewell.

Source

Richardson, ed. *Messages and Papers of the Presidents,* III, 292–308.

DOCUMENT 10

JACKSON COMMENTS ON TEXAS ANNEXATION

FEBRUARY 12, 1843

Jackson believed that the U.S. had a rightful claim to Texas, but John Quincy Adams had surrendered that claim in the Adams-Onís Treaty of 1819, by which the U.S. acquired Florida in exchange for a western boundary along the Louisiana border. Soon thereafter, both Adams and Jackson attempted unsuccessfully to purchase Texas from Mexico. The Lone Star Republic, independent since 1837, now faced threats from European influence that would do far more than limit America's continental destiny. Jackson paints a dire scenario of war, invasion, and slave rebellion if annexation is not accomplished.

But I forbear to dwell on this part of the history of the question. It is past and cannot now be undone. We can now only look at it as one of annexation, and if Texas presents it to us; and if she does, I do not hesitate to say that the welfare and happiness of our Union require that it should be accepted. If, in a military point of view alone, the question be examined, it will be found to be most important to the United States to be in possession of that territory. Great Britain has already made treaties with Texas, and we know that farseeing nation never omits a circumstance, in her extensive intercourse with the world which can be turned to account in increasing her military resources. May she not enter into a military alliance with Texas? And reserving, as she doubtless will, the northwestern boundary question as the cause of war with us whenever she chooses to declare it, let us suppose that, as an ally with Texas, we are to fight her!

Preparatory to such a movement, she sends 20,000 to 30,000 men to Texas, organizes them along the Sabine, where her supplies and arms can be concentrated even before we have even notice of her intentions; makes a lodgment on the Mississippi, excites the Negroes to insurrection, the lower country falls, and with it, New Orleans; and a servile war rages through the whole South and West.

In the meanwhile, she is also moving an army along the western frontier from Canada, which, in cooperation with the army from Texas, spreads ruin and havoc from the Lakes to the Gulf of Mexico. . . .

Remember, also, that if annexed to the United States, our western boundary would be the Rio Grande, which is itself a fortification on account of its extensive, barren, and uninhabitable plains. With such a barrier on our west we are invincible. The whole European world could not in combination against us, make an impression on our Union. Our population on the Pacific would rapidly increase and soon be strong enough for the protection of our Eastern whalers . . .

I must say that, in all aspects, the annexation of Texas to the United States promises to enlarge the circle of free institutions, and is essential to the United States, particularly lessening the probabilities of future collision with foreign powers, and giving them greater efficiency in spreading the blessings of peace.

Source

Andrew Jackson, February 12, 1843, to Aaron V. Brown, in James Parton, ed., *Life of Andrew Jackson,* (New York: Mason Brothers, 1860), III, 658–60.

BIBLIOGRAPHY

Adams, Sean P., ed. *A Companion to the Era of Andrew Jackson*. Malden, MA: Blackwell, 2013.
Bartlett, Irving. *John C. Calhoun*. New York: W.W. Norton, 1993.
Belohlavek, John M. "Assault on the President: The Jackson-Randolph Affair of 1833," *Presidential Studies Quarterly* XII, Summer 1982.
———. *Let the Eagle Soar!: The Foreign Policy of Andrew Jackson*. Lincoln: University of Nebraska Press, 1985.
Borneman, Walter R. *Polk: The Man Who Transformed the Presidency*. New York: Random House, 2008.
Brands, H.W. *Andrew Jackson: His Life and Times*. New York: Anchor Books, 2006.
Buell, A.C. *History of Andrew Jackson*. 2 vols. New York: Charles Scribner's Sons, 1904.
Burstein, Andrew. *The Passions of Andrew Jackson*. New York: A.A. Knopf, 2003.
Cheathem, Mark R. *Andrew Jackson: Southerner*. Baton Rouge: Louisiana State University Press, 2013.
Cole, Donald B. *The Presidency of Andrew Jackson*. Lawrence: University Press of Kansas, 1993.
Dennett, Tyler. *Americans in Eastern Asia*. New York: MacMillan, 1922.
Ellis, Richard. *The Union at Risk: Jacksonian Democracy, States' Rights, and the Nullification Crisis*. New York: Oxford University Press, 1987.
Heidler, David and Jeanne T. *Old Hickory's War: Andrew Jackson and the Quest for Empire*. Mechanicsburg, PA: Stackpole Books, 1996.
———. *Indian Removal*. New York: Norton, 2007.
Howe, Daniel Walker. *What Hath God Wrought: The Transformation of America, 1815–1848*. New York: Oxford University Press, 2007.
James, Marquis. *The Life of Andrew Jackson*. New York: Bobbs-Merrill, 1938.
Kendall, Amos. *The Life of Andrew Jackson*. New York: 1843.
Long, David F. "Martial Thunder: The First Official American Armed Intervention in Asia," *Pacific Historical Review*, 42, 1973.
Malone, Dumas. *Jefferson the President: First Term, 1801–1805*, Boston: Little Brown, 1970.
Marszalek, John. *The Petticoat Affair: Manners, Mutiny, and Sex in Andrew Jackson's White House*. New York: Free Press, 1997.
Meacham, Jon. *American Lion: Andrew Jackson in the White House*. New York: Random House, 2008.
Miller, William Lee. *Arguing about Slavery: John Quincy Adams and the Great Battle in the United States Congress*. New York: Random House, 1995.

Niven, John. *John C. Calhoun and the Price of Union.* Baton Rouge: Louisiana State University Press, 1988.

Niven, John. *Martin Van Buren and the Romantic Age of American Politics* (New York: Oxford University Press, 1983).

Parks, E.T. *Colombia and the United States.* Durham: Duke University Press, 1935.

Parton, James. *The Life of Andrew Jackson.* 3 vols. New York: Mason Brothers, 1860.

Reid, J. and J.H. Eaton. *The Life of Andrew Jackson.* Philadelphia: M. Carey, 1817.

Remini, Robert. *The Election of Andrew Jackson.* Philadelphia: J.B. Lippincott, 1963.

———. *Andrew Jackson and the Bank War.* New York: W.W. Norton, 1967.

———. *Andrew Jackson and the Course of American Empire, 1767–1821.* New York: Harper and Row, 1977.

———. *Andrew Jackson and the Course of American Freedom, 1822–1832.* New York: Harper and Row, 1981.

———. *Andrew Jackson and the Course of American Democracy, 1833–1845.* New York: Harper and Row, 1984.

Richardson, James D. *A Compilation of the Messages and Papers of the Presidents,* 10 vols. Washington: Government Printing Office, 1904.

Rives, George. *The United States and Mexico, 1821–1848.* New York: Scribner, 1913.

Silbey, Joel. *Martin Van Buren and the Emergence of American Popular Politics.* New York: Rowman and Littlefield, 2002.

Silbey, Joel. *Storm over Texas: The Annexation Controversy and the Road to Civil War.* New York: Oxford University Press, 2005.

Smith, S.B. Owsley, H.C., Moser, Harold, McPherson Sharon, and Feller, Daniel, eds. *The Papers Of Andrew Jackson.* Vols. 1–9. Knoxville: University of Tennessee Press, 1980–2013.

Stewart, James Brewer. *William Lloyd Garrison and the Challenge of Emancipation.* Arlington Heights, IL: Harlan Davidson, 1992.

Thomas, Robert C. "Andrew Jackson versus France," *Tennessee Historical Quarterly,* 35, 1976.

Washington Post. Political Science Association Poll, February 16, 2015.

Wilentz, Sean. *The Rise of American Democracy: From Jefferson to Lincoln.* New York: W.W. Norton, 2005a.

———. *Andrew Jackson.* New York: Times Books, 2005.

INDEX

Adams-Onis Treaty (Transcontinental Treaty) 40, 41, 42, 113, 143
Adams, John Quincy 35, 39–40, 47, 69, 92, 101, 102, 106; 1828 presidential campaign 56, 57, 58; 1923 presidential campaign 48, 51, 52, 53, 54; presidency 54, 55
Adams, Louisa Catherine 51
African Americans: and the Battle of New Orleans 30 *see also* slavery
Alabama 25–6
Allison, David 14, 17
Ambrister, Robert 36–7, 40, 41, 84–5
Amelia Island 34, 35
American exceptionalism 119
American Revolution 13
Anti-Masonic Party 72, 73, 79
Arbuthnot, Alexander 36–7, 40, 41, 84–5
Armstrong, John 24
Asia, trade with 97, 103
assaults on Andrew Jackson 91–5 *see also* duels fought by Andrew Jackson
assimilation, of Native Americans 42
Atlantic and Pacific Transportation Company 100
Avery, Waightstill 12

Bank of the United States (BUS): Bank Wars 75–8, 86–91, 134–6 *see also* First Bank of the United States
Barbour, Philip 94
Barry, William 65, 66, 86
Battle of New Orleans 2, 109
Battle of Tallushatchee 27

Battle of the Thames 27, 107
Benton, Jesse 25
Benton, Thomas Hart 25, 51, 55, 84–5, 105, 117
Berrien, John 65
Biddle, Charles 99, 100
Biddle, Nicholas 76–7, 86, 87, 88, 89–90, 91, 134
Birney, James G. 113
Black Hawk War, 1832 69
Blair, Francis P. 57
Blount, William 13, 14, 15, 17
Brackenridge, Henry 45, 46
Branch, John 65
Brands, H.W. 3
Britain 111, 112, 119–20; dumping of products 74; Jay Treaty 15; Napoleonic War 16, 23, 29; trade agreements with 97; trading and military posts 13; U.S. wars with 9–10, 23, 28–30, 31, 32
Bronaugh, James C. 45, 46
Burr, Aaron 20–1, 23, 56
Burstein, Andrew 3, 14
Butler, Anthony Wayne 49, 102
Butler, Robert 45
Butler, Thomas 20–1

Calhoun, Floride 65, 67
Calhoun, John C. 34, 35, 39, 42–3, 48, 50, 52, 57, 63, 66, 69, 73, 74, 75, 85, 89, 105, 112, 117, 119; split with Jackson 67–9
California 102, 112
Call, Richard 48, 51
Callava, José Maria 45, 46–7

Camden 9, 10
Campbell, George Washington 24
Canada: British colonial power in 13, 23, 29, 111; U.S. attacks on 24–5, 26–7
Carey, Mathew 32
Carroll, William 25
Cass, Lewis 86, 88
Central America, trade with 99–100
Charleston 9, 82–3, 85
Cheathem, Mark 3
Chehaw Indians 28
Cherokee Indians 3, 34, 70, 71, 72
Cherokee Nation v. Georgia 70
Chickasaw Indians 34, 43
Chile, trade with 99
China 99
Chinn, Julia 110
Choctaw Indians 30, 34, 71, 72
Claiborne, William C 20, 21
Clay, Henry 41, 42, 57, 58, 66, 69, 73, 75, 77, 78, 79, 85, 89, 91, 101, 105, 111, 112, 118; presidential candidacy 48, 49, 52, 54, 72, 113
Clayton-Bulwer Treaty, 1850 100
Clinton, Sir Henry 9
Coffee, John 49, 50, 75, 86
Colombia, trade with 99–100
commerce, Jackson's policy on 97–101
Committee on Military Affairs, House of Representatives 41
Compromise of 1819–1821 44
Cornwallis, Lord 9
corruption, Jackson's policy on 63–4, 117
Crawford, Jane (aunt of Andrew Jackson) 8
Crawford, Robert 9
Crawford, William H. 39, 41, 42, 63, 69; presidential candidacy 44, 48, 49, 50, 51, 52, 53
Creek Indians 2, 23, 24, 25–6, 29–30, 36
Cuba 50
cultural genocide, of Native Americans 43
Cumberland Road 44
Curtis, James C. 3
Cushing, Caleb 99

Dallas, Alexander J. 33
Dallas, George M. 83
Davie, Major William 99
Dearborn, Henry 21
Democratic Party 68, 117; 1832 presidential campaign 72–3, 79; and the Bank War 77, 90; and foreign policy 98; and the Removal Act, 1830 70

Denmark, spoliations payments 100
Deposit Bill 1836 90, 108
Dickinson, Charles 19–20, 21, 55, 123–4
Donelson Robards, Rachel *see* Jackson, Rachel
Donelson, Andrew Jackson 43–4, 65, 66, 93, 108
Donelson, Emily 65, 66, 108
Donelson, John 12
Downes, John 97–8
Driftwood, Jimmy 32
Duane, William J. 87–8
duels fought by Andrew Jackson: with Charles Dickinson 19–20, 21, 55, 123–4; with John Sevier 17–18; with Waightstill Avery 12

Eaton, John Henry 2, 32, 51, 55; and the Petticoat Affair 65–7
Eaton, Margaret (Margaret O'Neale Timberlake) 65–7 *see also* O'Neale, Margaret
Erwin, Joseph 19
Europe: changing attitudes to the U.S. 101, 103; as a threat to the U.S. 49–50

Far East, trade with 98–9
First Bank of the United States 75 *see also* Bank of the United States (BUS)
First Seminole War 36, 119
fiscal policy, of Jackson 87
Florida: Adams-Onis Treaty (Transcontinental Treaty) 40, 41, 42, 113, 143; Jackson's governorship of 45–7; Spanish colonial power in 23, 29–30, 34–7, 39–40
Floyd, John 79, 84, 93, 94
Force Bill 85
foreign affairs 112; Jackson's policy on 56, 96–103, 118
Forsyth, John 96
France, spoliations payments 100–1
franchise, extension of 3, 58, 116
Friedman, Michael 2
Ft. McHenry 29

Gadsby's Hotel 51, 53
Gaines, General Edmund P. 35
Gallatin, Albert 16
Garrison, William Lloyd 82
Gates, General Horatio 9
Georgia 84
gold prospecting 71
Greeley, Horace 3

Halcyon plantation 111
Hamilton, Alexander 74
Hamilton, James 83
Hamilton, James Jr. 75
Hampton, Wade 25
Harris, Egbert 19
Harrison, William Henry 25, 26–7, 28–9, 107, 110
Harvard University 92
Hayne, Robert Y. 84
Hemings, Sally 91
Hermitage, The 18, 20, 42, 43, 49, 61, 62; Jackson's retirement at 105–14; management of by Andrew Jackson Jr. 81–2, 108; as a visitor attraction 1, 116
Heston, Charlton 1–2
Hickory Tree, The 78
Hill, Isaac 92
Horseshoe Bend 26
Horton, Johnny 2, 32
Houston, Sam 47, 55, 102, 112
Howe, Daniel Walker 91
Humphries, William 8
Hunter's Hill plantation 14, 18
Hunters of Kentucky, The 125–6
Hutchings, Andrew Jackson 27, 58

Indians *see* Native Americans
Ingham, Samuel 65
internal improvements, Federal involvement in 44, 73; Jackson's policy on 55–6, 63, 68–9
Iturbide, Augustín de 49

Jackson, Andrew: assaults on 91–5; biographers of 2–3; cartoon portrayals of 132–3, 139–40; censure of, 1818–1819 39–40; character and personality of 3–4, 7–8, 120; death of 114; early military activity 9–10; early political career 14–16; early years (1767–1811) 7–21; education of 8; family background 8; Farewell Address 107, 141–2; first presidential term 1829–1833 61–79, 127–8; fiscal policy 87; foreign affairs policy 56, 96–103, 118; and gambling 11, 19; governorship of Florida 45–7; health issues 40, 47, 55, 57, 73, 92, 107, 108, 109, 111, 113–14; internal improvements policy 55–6, 63, 68–9; legacy of 116–20; legal career of 11–14, 17, 18; marriage to Rachel Donelson Robards 13–14 (*see also* Jackson, Rachel Donelson Robards); and the Petticoat Affair 65–7, 118; portrayals

of in popular culture 1–2, 31–2, 78–9, 125–6; prejudices of 3–4, 118–20; presidential campaign, 1821–1825 47–8, 50–4; presidential campaign, 1828 56–8; presidential campaign, 1832 72–3, 78–9; reputation of 1–2, 31–2, 33, 44–5, 51, 56–7, 105; retirement years 105–14; second presidential term 1833–1837 81–103, 105–6 *see also* duels fought by Andrew Jackson; military career of Andrew Jackson; Native Americans, Jackson's attitude towards; slavery, Jackson's attitude towards; tariffs, Jackson's policy on; Texas, Jackson's policy on
Jackson, Andrew III (son of Andrew Jackson Jr.) 82
Jackson, Andrew Jr. (nephew of Andrew Jackson) 21, 27, 33, 45, 58, 81–2, 108, 111
Jackson, Elizabeth (mother of Andrew Jackson) 8, 9, 10, 57
Jackson, Hugh (brother of Andrew Jackson) 8, 9
Jackson, Rachel (daughter of Andrew Jackson Jr.) 82
Jackson, Rachel Donelson Robards (wife of Andrew Jackson) 2, 10, 12, 13–14, 16, 43, 50–1; attitude to wars of 1812–1818 24, 27; death of 61–2, 118; distress at separation from Andrew Jackson 50–1; impact of the death of Lyncoya on 58, 61; life in Florida 45–6; life in New Orleans 33; reputation of 17–18, 19, 20, 56–7, 62, 91, 118
Jackson, Robert (brother of Andrew Jackson) 8, 9, 10
Jackson, Samuel 21
Jackson, Sarah 82, 108
Japan 99
Jay Treaty 15
Jefferson, Thomas 1, 16, 20, 21, 27, 65, 69, 75, 91, 118
Johnson, Richard M. 107, 110
Jonesborough 11–12

Kendall, Amos 57, 63–4, 77, 87, 92, 106
Kennedy, John F. 95
Kentucky, cession of Native American land 43
Key, Francis Scott 29

Lafitte, Jean 2, 30
Lawrence, Richard 94–5
Lewis, William B. 24, 55

Lincoln, Abraham 1
Livingston, Edward 86, 96
Louisiana Purchase 44, 113
Lumpkin, Wilson 71
Lyncoya 27, 58, 61

Madison, James 20, 21, 23, 32–3, 75
Maine 44, 111, 112
Mangum, Willie P. 107
Manifest Destiny 96, 112
Manrique, Governor Mateo Gonzalez 29–30
Marshall, John 62, 76, 94
martial law, in New Orleans 32–3
Mason, Jeremiah 76
Masonic Order 14, 72 *see also* Anti-Masonic Party
McCay, Spruce 11
McCulloch v. Maryland 76
McLane, Louis 85, 86, 87, 88, 96
McNairy, John 11
Meacham, Jon 3, 91
Mesquakie Indians 69
Mexican-American War, 1846 103
Mexico 48–9, 99, 119
Middle East, trade with 97
Mihm, Stephen 76
military career of Andrew Jackson: 1779–1781 period 9–10; 1812–1818 period 23–37; as commander of the Southern Division 34–7; as major-general of Tennessee 17, 21, 23
Mississippi, cession of Native American land 43
Missouri, slavery in 44
Mobile 29
Monroe Doctrine 50, 56
Monroe, James 21, 30, 34, 36, 37, 39, 40–1, 42, 46, 47, 48, 63
Morgan, Charles 100
Muscat 99

Naples, spoliations payments 100
Napoleonic War 16, 23, 29, 100
Nashville 14
National Party 71
National Republicans: 1828 presidential campaign 57; 1832 presidential campaign 72, 73, 79; and the Bank War 77, 78, 86, 119; and foreign policy 98; and the Removal Act, 1830 70
National Road, Kentucky 68–9

Native Americans: Jackson's attitude towards 2, 3, 14, 27–8, 43, 55, 69–72, 119, 129–31; removal of 3, 28, 34, 42–3, 55, 69–72, 84, 129–31
Negro Fort 35, 37
New England 23
New Orleans 24, 30–3
newspapers, and the 1928 presidential campaign 57–8
nullification 67, 71–2, 82–6, 137–8
Nullification Proclamation 83

O'Neale, Margaret 51 *see also* Eaton, Margaret
O'Neale, William 51, 53
Onis, Don Luis de 39, 40, 41
Oregon 112
Overton, John 12, 55, 86

Packenham, General Edward 31
Panama Congress, 1826 56
Panic of 1819 74, 76
Panic of 1837 90, 91, 108, 109
Parton, James 66–7
Peace of Paris 13
Pensacola 29–30, 34, 37
Perry, Matthew 99
Person, Benjamin 18
Peru-Bolivia, trade with 99
'pet banks' 88, 90
Petticoat Affair 65–7, 118
Pinckney, Charles Cotesworth 21
Poindexter, George 94
Poinsett, Joel 82, 109
Polk, James K. 110, 113
Poll (pet parrot) 62, 114
Portugal, spoliations payments 100

Quallah Battoo 97–8, 99
Quincy, Josiah 92

Rabun, William 28
Randolph, Robert B. 92–3, 95
recession of 1833–34 88
Reid, John 2, 32
Remini, Robert V. 2–3, 7, 27, 32, 89, 90–1, 109
Removal Act, 1830 70, 129–31
Rhea, John 36
Ridge, John 71
Ritchie, Thomas 57
Rives, William 100
Roane, Archibald 17

Robards, Lewis (first husband of Rachel Donelson Robards Jackson) 12, 13–14
Robert, Edmund 97, 98–9
Rogin, Michael Paul 3
Roosevelt, Franklin D. 1
Ross, John 71
Russia, trade with 97

Salisbury, North Carolina 11
Sauk Indians 69
Scott, Colonel Winfield 26
secession 83–4
Second Bank of the United States: Bank Wars 75–8, 86–91, 134–6
Second Seminole War 69
security, and the presidency 95
Seminoles 28, 34–5, 40, 69, 71
Sergeant, John 73
Sevier, John 17–18, 21
Shaker community, Lexington 42
Shawnee Indians 23, 26–7
Sheen, Martin 2
Siam 99
slavery: by Cherokee Indians 70; conflict over 44, 82, 106, 112; Jackson's attitude towards 2, 11–12, 13, 18–19, 43, 106, 107, 119
Smith, Margaret Baynard 63, 127–8
Smith, Samuel 112
South Carolina 71–2, 75, 82–3, 84–5, 112, 137
Spain: Adams-Onis Treaty (Transcontinental Treaty) 40, 41, 42, 113, 143; American colonies 12–13, 23, 29–30, 34–7, 39–40, 50; spoliations payments 100
Specie Circular 90, 106, 108
spoils system 64 *see also* corruption
St. Marks 36, 37
Steele, Graves 18
Stono Ferry 9
suffrage, extension of 3, 58, 116
Superior Court, Jackson's appointment to 17
Swartout, Samuel 65

Taney, Roger B. 77, 86, 87, 88
tariffs 71, 83; Jackson's policy on 56, 63, 67, 73–5, 82, 85–6; Tariff of 1816 67; Tariff of Abominations 67, 74
Tarleton, Colonel Banastre 9
Tecumseh, Shawnee chieftain 26–7, 29, 107

Tennessee, cession of Native American land 43
Texas 112–13; Jackson's policy on 101–3, 143–4; Spanish colonial power in 40
Third Seminole War 69
Timberlake, John 65, 92
Timberlake, Margaret *see* Eaton, Margaret (Margaret O'Neale Timberlake)
Timbers, Alex 2
'Trail of Tears' 3, 72
Transcontinental Treaty (Adams-Onis Treaty) 40, 41, 42, 113, 143
Treaty of Doak's Stand 43
Treaty of Fort Jackson 28
Treaty of New Echota 71
Treaty Party 71
Turkey, trade with 97
Turner, Nat 44, 82
Tyler, John 110, 111

Unionists 82

Van Buren, Martin 57, 64–5, 66, 67, 73, 74, 77, 84, 96, 106–7, 112–13, 117; presidency of 72, 107, 108, 109–10
Vanderbilt, Cornelius 100
Venezuela, trade with 99
Vietnam 99

Walton, Ira 19
War of 1812 2, 17, 25–6, 31, 33–4, 113
Washington, George 1, 15, 34
Webster-Ashburton Treaty, 1842 111–12
Webster, Daniel 57, 78, 85, 89, 101, 107, 111–12
Whigs 89, 101, 106, 107, 113
White, Hugh Lawson 107
Wilentz, Sean 3
Wilkinson, James 20–1, 24
Williams, John 50
Wirt, William 47, 72, 79
Woodbury, Levy 86, 98, 100
Woodworth, Samuel 125–6
Worcester v. Georgia 70
Worcester, Samuel 70, 71
Wright, Silas Jr. 74

Yorke, Sarah (Sarah Jackson) 82